D1557808

ST. PETER DAMIAN

THE BOOK OF GOMORRAH

THE BOOK OF GOMORRAH

AND

ST. PETER DAMIAN'S STRUGGLE AGAINST ECCLESIASTICAL CORRUPTION

Translated and Annotated
with Biographical Introduction
by Matthew Cullinan Hoffman

ITE AD THOMAM BOOKS AND MEDIA

NEW BRAUNFELS, TEXAS

www.iteadthomam.com

Cover art:

Center page: "The Dammed in Hell" from the Biblia Pauperum (1395–1400), Kings MS 5 fol. 31r. Courtesy of the British Library.

Lower page: Silhouette of the monastery of Fonte Avellana.

Cover design by Israel Aguilar Ortíz.

ISBN 978-0-9967042-0-5

Library of Congress Control Number 2015949870

This work is dedicated first to the infinite and eternal God, Father, Son, and Holy Spirit, in gratitude for the immense and unspeakable mercy He has shown me throughout my life, and in the hope that this work might be pleasing to Him. Second, it is dedicated to the Supreme Pontiff, Pope Francis, to all of his successors, and to all of the prelates of the Catholic Church, that they might heed the counsel of St. Peter Damian and fulfill their solemn duty to protect and preserve the moral and doctrinal integrity of the clergy and laity.

CONTENTS

FOREWORD

Saint Peter Damian (1007–1072) is the author of the *Book of Gomorrah*, which he dedicated to Pope Leo IX. In it he bluntly exposes and energetically condemns the immoral conduct of many Catholics of his time. Lax and poorly educated men, unworthy of their state, had infiltrated both the monasteries and the ranks of the secular clergy. Simony was practiced in the buying and selling of ecclesiastical offices, including the episcopacy. There was meddling by the civil authority in ecclesiastical affairs and in the nomination of abbots and bishops. The high dignitaries of the Church were often feudal lords, with the riches and the vices associated with such. Concubinage and marriage were common among the secular clergy and, even more sadly, with the approval of the faithful. And, as the saint says, the "cancer of sodomy," including pedophilia, had proliferated, above all in the monasteries.

Peter Damian forcefully and fearlessly denounced these evils, threatening the punishments of hell, and cried out to the pope for a reform that would purify the Church. He proposed disciplinary measures that were adopted by the Church, and some of them continue in effect in the law until today, although unfortunately they are not always applied.

Peter Damian was most eminent in his day: he was highly educated, a great theologian, bishop, cardinal of the Holy Church, and legate of various Supreme Pontiffs before princes and kings, but above all, he was a saint who contributed to the reform of the Church. Pope Saint Leo IX thanked Saint Peter Damian in a commemoratory letter regarding the *Book of Gomorrah* and vigorously undertook the reform of the customs of the Church, which, by the acts of this Pontiff and others who followed him, would be raised to its splendor in sanctity and knowledge during the 12th and 13th centuries.

The *Book of Gomorrah* has recently been translated from the original Latin into English, with copious introductory material, by an erudite Catholic who is faithful to Christ and his Church: Matthew Cullinan Hoffman. I have accepted with pleasure the task of writing this brief presentation of a book which, upon its reading, brings us to the realization that a thousand years ago sexual vices were being practiced by various sons of the Church that lamentably are present today and have been the occasion of scandal, discredit, and apostasy. Today, like then, with prayer and the example of the saints, and the firm hand of pastors, the sons of the Church can return to the way of faithfulness in order to fully carry out the mission of being "salt of the earth and the light of the world."

Juan Cardinal Sandoval Íñiguez
Archbishop Emeritus of Guadalajara

Guadalajara, Jalisco, June 30, 2015

ACKNOWLEDGMENTS

I would like to thank all of those mortal souls who contributed to this project, and in particular those who generously took the time and effort to analyze my work and offer helpful suggestions, comments, and endorsements, including His Eminence Juan Cardinal Sandoval Íñiguez, Archbishop Emeritus of Guadalajara, Msgr. Ignacio Barreiro, Executive Director of the Rome Office of Human Life International, Dr. Joseph Shaw, Tutorial Fellow in Philosophy at St. Benet's Hall, Oxford, Dr. Daniel Van Slyke, Associate Professor of Theology and Associate Dean of Online Learning at Holy Apostles College, Dr. Francisco Romero Carrasquillo, Associate Professor of Humanities at the Panamerican University, Guadalajara, Dr. Michela Ferri, Adjunct Professor of Philosophy at Holy Apostles College, and Fr. Shenan Boquet, President of Human Life International. I wish also to thank Israel Aguilar for his excellent cover design and patient edits thereof, and April Bright and Kevin Klump for their kind help with proofreading. Finally, I would like to express my profound gratitude to my mother, Margaret Hoffman, who supported this project financially, as well as offering her helpful expertise in English grammar and composition in the crucial final edits to the work. Without the generous support of these individuals and many others, this work would not have been possible.

INTRODUCTION

ST. PETER DAMIAN'S STRUGGLE AGAINST ECCLESIASTICAL CORRUPTION

A Church in Crisis

The great reformer who would become known to the world as Peter Damian was born into a troubled Italy and a troubled Church. When he first opened his eyes in the year 1007, Western Europe was in the last decades of its most obscure period, having suffered more than a century and a half of violent incursions of Vikings, Muslims, and Magyars. The region had fragmented into countless principalities, and trade and intellectual commerce had declined. The literary patrimony of Latin antiquity maintained a tenuous presence in the care of monasteries and diocesan libraries, which had been decimated by the marauding invaders.

During this tumultuous epoch Italy had been largely cut off from the stabilizing rule of the German emperors and had become an armed camp of fortified towns under the rule of local strongmen, constantly on the defense against attacks by invaders as well as one another. The papacy had also become embroiled in the anarchy of the time, as the popes, who had ruled the city of Rome since the sixth century, became power brokers and ultimately pawns in the political infighting that convulsed the peninsula.

The precipitous decline of the papacy had begun after the deposition in 887 of Charlemagne's great-grandson, Charles the Fat, the last of a line of Carolingian kings who had protected the papacy and held the title of Roman Emperor. With the end of Charles's reign, the empire that had been erected by Charlemagne, stretching from the Pyrenees to the Elbe river and encompassing half of Italy, collapsed in all but name. Pope Stephen VI (885–91) gave the title of emperor, and therefore the rule of Italy, to the Italian Guido III, duke of the neighboring territory of Spoleto. However, Stephen's successor, Pope Formosus (891–96), favored Guido's Frankish rival, Arnulf of Carinthia, crowning him as Emperor instead. The battle over the throne of Italy then became a vindictive rivalry between kingmaker popes, as Formosus's successor, the pro-Spoletan Stephen VII (896–97), had his predecessor's body disinterred and put on trial for the purpose of declaring him an antipope and invalidating all of his ordinations and acts of governance.

The tit-for-tat between the two parties continued for a decade, with Pope Theodore II (897) confirming the papacy of Formosus and nullifying his condemnation by Stephen, a verdict confirmed by his successor, John IX (898–900), and in turn reinforced by Benedict IV (900–03), who crowned the German king Louis the Blind as emperor. However, after Benedict's successor was violently deposed and imprisoned, the pro–Spoletan Sergius III (904–11) in turn deposed his predecessor and again nullified the tenure of Formosus and all of his ordinations.[1]

---

[1] The issue was ultimately resolved by canonists in favor of Formosus, who is today generally recognized as a valid pope, despite the final negative judgment by Sergius III.

The battle over the papacy (and the body) of Pope Formosus was devastating for the Holy See and the Italian church. The illegal acts of Stephen VII and Sergius III, and the political rivalry of the popes who opposed them, could only undermine respect for papal authority and cast into doubt the validity of the ordinations of countless bishops and priests. The popes had politicized the papacy by appropriating its spiritual functions for secular ends. However, the shameful affair was merely a prelude to decades of instability, violence, and corruption, as rival factions of the Roman elite vied for control of the city and the ecclesiastical regime that governed it.

In 928 the Roman noblewoman Marozia, daughter of papal kingmakers Count Theophylact of Tusculum and his wife Theodora, had the illustrious Pope John X deposed and imprisoned, whereupon he quickly died.[2] She soon placed a young son (rumored to also be the illegitimate offspring of Pope Sergius III) on the papal throne as John XI (931–35). After Marozia and her faction was overthrown by her disowned son, Alberic II, Pope John XI was converted into a political protégé of the latter, as were his successors Leo VII (936–39), Stephen IX (939–42), Marinus II (942–46), and Agapetus II (946–55). Finally, following the death of Alberic, his eighteen-year-old son, Octavius, was elected Pope John XII (955–63). We are told by commentators of the time that

---

[2] Pope John is reported by the chronicler Liutprand, Bishop of Cremona (in his *Antapadosis*, lib. 2, cap.48; PL 136, 827D–828C), to have been the lover of Marozia's mother Theodora before ascending the papal throne, but as a very hostile commentator who was not alive at the time of the events in question, his accounts of this period of the papacy are not regarded as credible by historians.

John "lived in a pigsty of lust,"[3] which was so scandalous that a synod of bishops was called to treat the problem, and an antipope was unsuccessfully named to replace him.[4] He died shortly after deposing and mutilating his rival and restoring himself to power at the age of 26.[5]

The turmoil in the papacy continued following the restoration of the imperial title in 962 under the Saxon king Otto I, who began to rein in the recalcitrant Italian aristocracy by supporting his own papal candidates. A century more of sometimes violent conflict over the papacy would follow, which only slowly subsided as Otto and his successors began to subdue the chaotic mess that was northern and central Italy. The popes continued to function as the temporal rulers of Rome but were now perceived as political vassals of the German emperors, who in turn depended upon the popes for their own imperial title. The dynamics of this symbiotic relationship were often confused with the spiritual power of the papacy, which in theory remained distinct and independent of the secular power.

Although the official acts of the popes of this period were generally unobjectionable and often laudable, their

[3] This statement is reported in an account attributed to Gerbert of Aurillac, later Pope Sylvester II, in the *Acta Concilii Remensis*, cap. 28 (PL 139, 313B).

[4] This synod was held in Rome in 963 under the auspices of Emperor Otto I. Although it appears to be a response to the morally scandalous behavior of John XII, its decision to depose the pope is generally regarded as illegal.

[5] Liutprand, Bishop of Cremona, in his *De Rebus Gestis Ottonis*, cap. 20 (PL 136, 908D), famously claims that John died several days after being "struck in the temples by the devil" while in the act of adultery, and that he refused Holy Communion until the end. However, Liutprand was an opponent of John who had participated in the council that sought to depose him, and is the only one to report the story.

compromised situation and poor personal example had combined with the vicissitudes of the age to provoke a catastrophic decline in clerical morality. The ranks of the monasteries and secular priesthood had been adulterated with lax and uneducated men, unworthy of their office. Corruption was rife, and the offices of the clergy, including bishoprics, were often sold. Many priests violated the Church's strictures against sacerdotal marriage by entering into illicit unions with wives or concubines, with the consent and even the approval of their flocks. Large numbers had succumbed to unnatural sexual practices, alone or with others, all of which fell under the dread name of "sodomy," in reference to the city of Sodom destroyed by God in the book of Genesis.

Peter Damian's Early Life

The traditional account of Peter's infancy serves as yet another reminder of the harsh conditions of the period. According to his first biographer, John of Lodi,[6] the future saint was born into a noble but impoverished family in Ravenna, a city that had long functioned as the conduit between the Byzantine empire and the city of Rome. Following an older son's complaint of a diminished inheritance and a crowded home, his mother refused to breastfeed the newborn until the wife of a priest scolded her to shame. However, both of Peter's parents soon died, and the young child found himself in the custody of a cruel older brother and his concubine, who abused him

[6] John of Lodi was a monk of Fonte Avellana and close confidant of the saint, who would ultimately be canonized as well. He is generally supposed to be the "John" who authored Damian's first and most authoritative biography (found in *Gaetani*, vol. 1, 1–16), although this cannot be verified with absolute certainty.

physically and treated him like a slave, forcing him to work as a swineherd.[7]

The young Peter was finally delivered from his tormentors by another brother, Damian, who "embraced him with such dear affection, cared for him so diligently, that he would seem to have exceeded parental affection," according to St. John of Lodi.[8] Damian sent his younger brother to the cities of Faenza and Parma to be instructed by the best teachers of grammar and liberal arts, in which he excelled. The young Peter's immense gratitude and love for his beneficent older sibling led him to take his first name as a surname, becoming *Petrus Damiani*, meaning "Peter of Damian."[9] Peter's brother had become a second father to him, in a profound act of mercy that would inadvertently immortalize his name.

Peter's abilities amazed his teachers, according to his biographer, and following the completion of his studies he became a renowned professor of liberal arts, which earned him great respect and subjected him to worldly temptations. Students flocked to him, attracted by his great oratorical gifts and the depth of his learning. However, it was at this time that the saint began to meditate on the transience of worldly pleasures and the abiding value of the spiritual and divine, to "aspire to be removed from mundane studies, and to be girded with divine service," and although he "appeared to adhere to perishable things through the splendor of external refinement, yet with

[7] To this account must be added (or substituted) Peter's own statement, made in a letter to the Empress Agnes, that following his parents' death he was cared for at some point by a sister who "nurtured me like a mother" (see Letter 149 in *Reindel*, vol. 3, 552).

[8] John of Lodi, *Vita Beati Petri Damiani*, cap. 2 (*Gaetani*, vol. 1, 3). Translation mine.

[9] Peter's surname was often written in the nominative case as well, as "Damianus."

all of his heart he sought after eternal goods."[10] He began to engage in ascetic and charitable practices, wearing a hairshirt under his expensive clothing, immersing himself in cold water when tempted by sexual desire, and feasting the poor with banquets at his own table.[11] Soon he decided to completely abandon the distractions of the secular life, joining the hermitage of Fonte Avellana many miles to the south of Ravenna, around the year 1035.

Damian embraced the rigorous asceticism of the hermitage, which was famous for extreme acts of penance, and devoted himself to spiritual learning. Although he at first exceeded the others in his penitential exercises, he was eventually forced to moderate his zeal when his practices provoked a severe illness. However, his great abilities as a scholar soon caught the attention of his superiors, who assigned him to preach to the other monks. As his fame grew, he was called to other monasteries as well, to teach Scripture and preach on the spiritual life. Upon the death of the prior of Fonte Avellana in 1043, Damian was elected as his successor and began to found other hermitages, sowing the seeds of a monastic order that would last until the sixteenth century.[12]

Upon his accession to the leadership of Fonte Avellana, Damian took up the reform of the hermitage in earnest. He established a library containing the works of Church Fathers as well as secular authors, purchased adequate vessels for the celebration of the Mass and other sacraments, and built a

---

[10] Lodi, *Vita*, cap. 2 (*Gaetani*, vol. 1, 3). Translation mine.

[11] Ibid.

[12] The order, which came to be known as Santa Croce di Fonte Avellana, was absorbed into the Camaldolese Order in 1570 after a period of decline.

cloister for communal meetings.[13] He busied himself with the spiritual edification of his brothers as well, calling them together often for instruction on topics pertaining to the religious life. As his reputation spread, he was increasingly called to visit other communities to aid them in their own reform. He was soon a ubiquitous presence in the monasteries of Italy, touring them frequently and inundating them with his writings.

Peter's zeal for reform now began to extend beyond the confines of the monasteries to the secular clergy and civil society, which had continued to languish under a politicized and sometimes corrupt papacy. After the death of Emperor Otto III in 1002 the imperial title had lain dormant for twelve years, until it was conferred upon the pious but politically weak German king Henry II, who was able to exert little influence over his Italian domains. During this period the papacy again had fallen into the hands of the Roman clan that had been led by Marozia and her son Alberic in the 10th century, now under the sway of the self-styled "patrician" John Crescentius. Following Crescentius' death in 1012, power had passed to the counts of nearby Tusculum, whose corrupting influence reached its culmination with the accession of Pope Benedict IX (1033–45), a youth of no more than 22 years of age.[14] Although the details of his scandalous behavior are unclear, sources from the period are unanimous in their

---

[13] Owen J. Blum, *St. Peter Damian: his teaching on the spiritual life* (Washington, D.C.: Catholic University of America Press, 1947), 14.

[14] The monk Rodulfus Glaber in his *Historiarum Libri Quinque*, lib. 4, cap. 5, reports that the young pope, whose given name was Theophylact, was only ten years of age at his accession, a claim that is generally rejected as untenable by historians. See *Raoul Glaber: les cinq Livres de ses histoires*, ed. Maurice Prou (Paris, 1886), 105.

condemnation of the young pontiff, who is accused of debauchery and murder.[15]

It was in the final year of the reign of Benedict IX that Damian first began to raise his voice against the corruption of the papacy. In a letter to Peter, the pope's chancellor, Damian writes with unflinching frankness about the abysmal state of the Holy See and its vital necessity as the source of the renewal of Christendom:

> Most beloved, as I am not ignorant of the situation in Rome and frequently hear about your character, my mind returns to this thought: that He who is able to produce the splendid lily in a thicket of thorns[16] wishes you to produce the same among the misdeeds of the Romans.... For unless the Roman see returns to the state of rectitude, it is certain that the whole world, having fallen into its error, will so remain. Moreover, it is necessary that that which once rose to become the foundation of human salvation, now become the source of renewal.[17]

When the dissolute Benedict was induced to resign with a monetary gift from the well-meaning John Gratian, who briefly succeeded him as Pope Gregory VI (1045–1046), Damian wrote to the new pontiff urging him to act against corruption

---

[15] Desiderius, abbot of Monte Cassino (who reigned as Pope Victor III from 1086–1087) in his *Dialogi*, cap. 3 (PL 149, 1003A–1004B), seems to offer the most detailed and credible description of Benedict IX's misbehavior, which he says he "dreads to report." He confines himself to mentioning Benedict's "vile and contemptible life," his "rapine, murders, and other nefarious deeds," and his "depraved and perverse acts" which he committed "unstintingly against the Roman people." He also accuses him of obtaining the papacy through bribery.

[16] Cf. Song of Sol. 2:2.

[17] Letter 11 in *Reindel*, vol. 1, 138–139. Translation mine.

in the Church, and in particular to remove the infamous bishop of the Italian city of Pesaro:

> Now may the multiform head of the poisonous serpent be crushed, and the commerce of perverse business come to an end. May the forger Simon cease to impress his coin in the Church, and may Giezi no longer carry away stolen gifts in the present absence of the prophetic doctor.[18] Now may the dove return to the ark, and with the green foliage of the olive tree, announce the return of peace to the nations.[19] Now may the golden age of the apostles be restored, and with your prudence presiding, may ecclesiastical discipline again flourish. May the avarice of those who struggle for the bishop's miter be repressed, and the seats of the money-changers selling doves be overturned.[20]
>
> However, whether it might be reasonable for the world to expect these things of which we write, the Church of Pesaro will first give a clear indication of good hope. For unless the aforesaid church is taken away from the hand of that incestuous adulterer, perjurer and robber, all the hope of the restoration of the world that has been raised among the peoples will be completely drained. Indeed, all turn their eyes to this purpose, all raise their ears to this one voice. And if that bishop, implicated in so many crimes, is restored to the height of the episcopacy, the

[18] Simon was a sorcerer who attempted to purchase sacramental powers from the apostle Peter (Acts 8:9–24) and Giezi was the servant of the prophet Elisha who deceitfully solicited payment for a miraculous healing (2 Kings 5:1–27). Both are seen in medieval literature as archetypes of those who seek material profit from spiritual goods, and hence the epithets "simony" and "simoniac."

[19] Cf. Gen. 8:11.

[20] Cf. Matt. 21:12–13; Luke 19:45–46; John 2:14–16.

Apostolic See will be utterly unable to do any further good.[21]

Although it is not known if Pope Gregory acted against the bishop of Pesaro, it is certain that he had little time to address the crisis in the Church, as he was convinced to resign in December of 1046 at a council of bishops held in Sutri, Italy, after admitting his bribe to Benedict IX. He was briefly succeeded by Pope Clement II, whose attempt to eliminate simony was cut short by his unexplained death while traveling through the same diocese of Pesaro. During Clement's brief pontificate Damian wrote to him as well, lamenting the state of "the churches of God, which in our parts are altogether confused by bad bishops and abbots," and asking "what good is it, my Lord, that we say that the Apostolic See has returned from darkness to light, if we still remain in the same darkness?"

> How does it help if someone places a vital supply of food under lock and key and yet perishes from hunger? What good is it if one is girded with the iron of an elegant sword, if it is not wielded against the surrounding battalions? For the omnipotent God put you in his place among the people in a certain sense as food, and through you he has armed his flank against all of the attacks of the enemies of his Church.... Therefore, most blessed lord, endeavor to raise up the justice that has been trampled and cast aside, thus apply the discipline of ecclesiastical vigor, so that the party of iniquity will be cast down from its place of arrogance, and the soul of the humble faithfully recover in anticipation of the good to come.[22]

---

[21] Letter 13 in *Reindel*, vol. 1, 143–144. Translation mine.

[22] Letter 26 in *Reindel*, vol. 1, 241–242.

Following Clement's death, the ever-conniving Benedict returned to rule Rome as an antipope in late 1047, until he was finally driven from the city in July of 1048.[23] The state of the papacy, and the Catholic Church as a whole, had reached what may be justly considered a historic nadir. St. Bruno, the reforming bishop of the Italian city of Segni, later summarized the situation:

> The whole world had fallen into malignity. Sanctity had disappeared, justice had perished, and truth had been buried. Evil reigned, avarice dominated. Simon Magus possessed the Churches. Priests did not blush to take wives, entering into abominable marriages and giving legitimacy to those with whom, according to the law, they must not even live together in a single house.... But worst of all, hardly any cleric could be found who was not a simoniac, or who had not been ordained by a simoniac.... Such was the Church, such were the bishops and priests, such were some of the Roman pontiffs, who had the obligation to enlighten everyone else. All salt had gone flat, and there was nothing with which it could be restored,[24] and if the Lord had not left us a seed, we would have been like Sodom and Gomorrah.[25,26]

It was at this terrible juncture that one of these "seeds" would ascend the papal throne and begin the great work of restoration longed for by Damian and other reformers. In response to the outcry against the corruption of the papacy, Emperor

[23] A legitimate pope, who took the name of Damasus II, held the see for a total of 23 days following the final removal of Benedict IX, having been consecrated on July 17 and dying on August 9.

[24] Cf. Luke 14:34.

[25] Cf. Rom. 9:29; Isa. 1:9.

[26] Bruno Signiensis, *S. Leonis Papae IX Vita* (PL 165, 1110B–1111B). Translation mine.

Henry III nominated Bruno von Egisheim, a German aristocrat and future saint who as Bishop of Toul[27] was already famous for his piety and holiness. He entered Rome in pilgrim's garb in February of 1049 and was elected to the papacy with the unanimous assent of the clergy and people, taking the name of Leo IX. He then set out upon one of the most phenomenal pontificates in history, traveling throughout Italy and Western Europe in an unremitting campaign against clerical and lay corruption, holding synods on the reform of the clergy in Rome, Papia, Rheims, and Mainz in the year 1049 alone.[28] Pope Leo had inaugurated an age of reform that would restore the reputation of the clergy and elevate the papacy to the height of power and influence in Europe.

Two Blows Against Corruption: The Book of Gomorrah and the "Most Gracious Book"

Damian saw no need for expostulating with the new pope regarding the corrupting influences of simony and clerical concubinage, problems that Leo began immediately to address with the greatest energy. However, through his experiences as a monastic reformer, Damian had become aware of an even more insidious and less-publicized crisis in the Church: that of the widespread practice of sodomy among clerics and monks. He responded with one of the most powerful works of his career, which would later be called the *Liber Gomorrhianus* or "Book of Gomorrah,"[29] and which he addressed to the new pontiff.

[27] The city is today in France, although it was part of the Holy Roman Empire until the 16th century.

[28] *Regesta Pontificum Romanorum*, ed. Philippus Jaffé (Berolini: Veit et Socius, 1851), 368–369.

[29] The title "Book of Gomorrah" only begins to appear in manuscripts during the fourteenth century. However, because it has been accepted

The work, which was written sometime between 1049 and 1054,[30] warns Leo that "a certain most abominable and exceedingly disgraceful vice has grown in our region, and unless it is quickly met with the hand of strict punishment, it is certain that the sword of divine fury is looming to attack, to the destruction of many." This terrible plague is "the cancer of sodomitic impurity," which "is creeping through the clerical order, and indeed is raging like a cruel beast within the sheepfold of Christ with the audacity of such liberty, that for many it would have been much more salutary to be oppressed by the yoke of worldly duties, than to be surrendered so freely to the iron rule of diabolical tyranny under the pretense of religion."[31]

Damian then proceeds to an eloquent and impassioned condemnation of various forms of sexual perversion, which he places under the heading of "sodomy," including contraception, masturbation, same-sex pederasty, and adult homosexual acts. He notes the severe penalties historically attached to such offenses in the Scriptures as well as the canons of Church councils, and argues that such penalties should be even stronger for members of the clergy, who are to be held to a higher standard than the laity. The strongest punishments in the Church's historic legislation are reserved for those who abuse children and adolescents. They are to be "publicly beaten" and humiliated, "bound in iron chains, worn down with six months of imprisonment, and three days every week

---

for centuries as the title of the work, I have chosen to retain it for this translation. The work appears as "Letter 31" in *Reindel*, vol.1, 284–330. See Translator's Preface for details.

[30] Reindel assigns this letter to the year 1049 (*Reindel*, vol. 1, 284), although it could have been written any time during the pontificate of Pope Leo IX (1049–1054).

[31] *Book of Gomorrah*, chapter 1.

to fast on barley bread at sundown," and confined to a monastery in perpetuity under constant guard.

The *Book of Gomorrah* describes in ringing prose the wretch-
edness of sodomy, which "surpasses the savagery of all other
vices," and causes "the death of bodies, the destruction of
souls, pollutes the flesh, extinguishes the light of the mind,
expels the Holy Spirit from the temple of the human heart,"
and "introduces the diabolical inciter of lust." It also expresses deep compassion for those who are consumed by
such self-destructive behavior, lamenting "the fall of the
eminent soul, and the destruction of the temple in which
Christ had dwelt." "May my eyes fail from weeping, may they
pour out abundant streams of tears, and may they water sad
and mournful expressions with continuous crying," Damian
writes, encouraging those who have fallen to repent, assuring
them that by the route of humility they may progress to even
greater spiritual heights than those from which they fell.

Pope Leo responded to the work with a letter of endorsement praising Damian to a degree seldom paralleled in papal
correspondence. Calling him "most beloved son," Leo declares that the work "commends the effort of your soul for
having reached, through pious struggle, the splendid nuptial
bed of shining chastity." He congratulates Damian for having
"raised the arm of the Spirit against the obscenity of lust,"
and rejoices that "whatever you have taught with your ability
as a preacher, you also teach through the example of your
life. For it is better to instruct by deed, than by word." "As a
result," promises Leo,

> you will obtain the palm of victory from God the Father,
> you will rejoice in the celestial mansion with the Son of
> God and of the Virgin, heaped up with as many rewards as

were taken by you from the snares of the devil, with which you will have been associated and in a sense, crowned."[32]

Leo accepts Damian's suggestion that punishments be meted out based on the degree of the sin, decreeing that those who have engaged in lesser degrees of sodomy infrequently and with few companions may recover their grade of priesthood after a suitable atonement, whereas those who have committed anal sodomy, or who have engaged in lesser degrees of sodomy for long periods of time or with many others, are to be permanently removed from the ranks of the clergy.

During the same pontificate, Damian turned his pen to a second grave scandal afflicting the priesthood: the widespread practice of "simony," or the buying and selling of ordinations, which were often associated with lucrative positions of leadership in the Church. Following a request made by Leo for opinions regarding the treatment of the problem, Damian responded with the *Liber Gratissimus* or "Most Gracious Book."[33] In the *Liber Gratissimus*, Damian denounces simony while defending the integrity of the sacrament of Holy Orders from the attacks of rigorists such as Humbert, Cardinal Bishop of Silva Candida, who called into question the validity and legality of ordinations carried out by those bishops who had paid to receive their own ordinations.[34] As Damian would later note in an appendix to the work, his position was ultimately upheld by Leo, who decreed that those ordained by simonists could continue in their offices following a brief penance and

[32] Leo IX's prediction would be confirmed in 1823, when Damian's feast day was made universal by Pope Leo XII, who also assigned to the saint the title of Doctor of the Catholic Church.

[33] Letter 40 in *Reindel*, vol. 1, 384–509.

[34] See *Humberti S.R.E. Cardinalis Adversus Simoniacos Libri Tres* (PL 143, 1007A–1212B).

without reordination. The popes would repeatedly affirm this verdict in the centuries to come.

Damian provided assistance to Leo's reform campaign by reinforcing his declarations condemning abuses and even acting as his official representative. In a letter written in Leo's name to the clergy and people of the diocese of Ostia, Damian roundly condemns their "execrable custom" of looting and destroying the home and property of deceased bishops. He declares on Leo's behalf, "in the name of the omnipotent God and by the authority of the blessed apostles Peter and Paul," that anyone guilty in the future of such "bestial savagery" is "to be anathematized, and we cut off such putrid members from the body of the holy Church with the sword of excommunication," unless they repent.[35] In another letter to the bishop of the same diocese, he presents arguments reinforcing Leo's condemnation of the practice of permitting monks to abandon their vows. "What is this insanity, what is this madness, what is this cruelty?" he writes. "Does a man have the liberty to freely dispose of his goods, but lacks the power to offer himself to God?"[36]

Damian was well aware of the dangers entailed in his opposition to the corruption of his day but would not be deterred, declaring in the *Book of Gomorrah*:

> I have sought with all zeal the favor of the interior Judge, but do not fear the hatred of the depraved or the tongues of detractors. Indeed, I prefer to be thrown innocent into a well with Joseph, who accused his brothers to their father of the worst of crimes, than to be punished by the

---

[35] Letter 35 in *Reindel*, vol. 1, 336–339. Translation mine.

[36] Letter 38 in *Reindel*, vol. 1, 352.

retribution of divine fury with Eli, who saw the evil of his children and was silent.[37]

The tongues of detractors were indeed soon turned against Damian, reaching the ears of Pope Leo himself. Writing to Leo, Damian decries a whispering campaign that was slandering him in response to his efforts at reform, and which he feared had influenced the pontiff:

> This, at least, I may say to my accusers, that the Israelite people said to their preachers, "The Lord see and judge, because you have made our savor to stink before Pharaoh and his servants."[38] For the ancient enemy, fearing that by my suggestions to you I might destroy that which he does not cease in this region to fabricate by new devices, has sharpened the tongues of the malignant against me, and his accomplices have made a certain individual into an organ for themselves for the purpose of composing lies, who has sounded through his pipes and has infused the poison of his malice into sacred ears. And how is it surprising if my lord, who is pressed by such cares, might have been influenced by the clever persuasiveness of men, when David also, who was filled with the prophetic spirit, rashly believed Siba and immediately condemned Miphiboseth with the sentence of confiscation?[39,40]

Reminding Leo that "we should not easily believe whatever evils" we hear of others, Damian encourages him to investigate the matter, expressing his willingness to accept whatever the pope might decide. No response from Leo is extant, and

[37] Chapter 26.

[38] Exod. 5:21.

[39] That is, he confiscated his goods and gave them to his servant Siba (2 Sam. 16:1–4).

[40] Letter 33 in *Reindel*, vol. 1, 332–333. Translation mine.

no reference is made to the matter in any of Damian's other writings. The paucity of available correspondence by Damian and other documentation dating from this period makes it impossible to determine precisely when the letter was written to Leo, as well as the ultimate outcome of the controversy, and historians differ widely in their assessment of the affair. However, if Damian's later reputation is any indication, it would seem that the matter was short-lived and relatively unimportant; despite any opposition he might have suffered, he was elevated to cardinalate by succeeding pontiffs, who called upon him repeatedly for assistance in a variety of important matters, finally raising him to second place in the Church of Rome, subject only to the pope himself.

Theologian and Activist

Damian would continue his campaign against ecclesiastical corruption with steely determination in the years and decades that followed, reserving some of his strongest admonitions for bishops and even popes who failed in their duty to protect and uphold justice and clerical morality. In 1057 he wrote to Pope Victor II as if he were quoting Christ himself, to rebuke him for failing to do justice for a monk who had been mistreated:

> I have placed the keys of the whole universal Church in your hands, and over that which I have redeemed by the spilling of my own blood, I placed you as my vicar.... I, however, who have given you such and so many things, do not find law or justice in your balance, and I depart from your tribunals despised and unavenged.[41]

---

[41] Letter 46 in *Reindel*, vol. 2, 41–42.

Striking again at the sexual immorality of the clergy, Damian wrote to Pope Nicholas II in 1059 urging him to act against sexually incontinent prelates, asking, "What worse thing can one do than to spare lustful bishops when he has the power to correct them?" He denounces the practice of covering up scandals among the clergy and warns the pontiff of divine punishment should he fail to carry out his duty in such matters:

> Clearly, just as those who punish faults are worthy of bless-ing, so those who coddle sinners are subject to a curse, as the prophet says: "Cursed be he that withholdeth his sword from blood."[42] Indeed, he who withholds his sword from blood is he who restrains himself from imposing the punishment of a proper sentence against evildoers. "Those who fail to correct are themselves guilty of the act."[43] If, therefore, Eli, only because of two sons whom he did not correct with a proper punishment, perished together with them and with such a great multitude of men, of what sentence do we think them to be worthy who preside in the palaces of the Church and in the seats of judgment, and who are silent in the face of the known offenses of depraved men?[44]

In 1064 Damian wrote on the same theme to Cunibert, the bishop of Turin, excoriating him for allowing his priests to mar-ry in defiance of the historic custom of the Church. "Read, O father, the letter on the incontinence of the clergy that I sent to

---

[42] Jer. 48:10.

[43] This sentence appears virtually verbatim in the *Decree of Gratian*, pars 1, dist. 86, c. 3, although Damian's source predates it by at least a century. In editions of the *Corpus Iuris Canonici* it has been attributed to a letter of Pope Gregory the Great, *Theodorico et Theoberto Regibus Francorum*, epist. 114, lib. 7, indict. 2.

[44] Letter 61 in *Reindel*, vol. 2, 212–213. Translation mine.

Pope Nicholas of pious memory, and whatever you might find written there on this topic, understand to be no less directed to you," writes Damian, who asks,

> Given that all of the holy Fathers, who established the canons by the Holy Spirit, without any dissent unanimously agree among themselves regarding the preservation of priestly chastity, what hope is there for those who blaspheme the Holy Spirit by fulfilling carnal enticements in their own flesh? Indeed, through the transience of momentary lust, they purchase the inextinguishable fire of eternal combustion. Now they soil themselves with the foulness of pleasure, later, turned over to vengeful flames, they will whirl in a torrent of tar and sulfur.[45]

Although he strongly opposed the laxism of his day, focusing his efforts on the correction and punishment of clerical corruption, Damian also opposed excessive rigor in punitive measures, writing to Pope Nicholas in 1059 to urge him to rescind an excommunication he was maintaining against the Italian city of Ancona, despite its efforts at reconciliation: "Far may it be from my lord, that while a tyrant is restrained by fear after cutting down only two or three men, the sword of him who is the master of all Christian mercy should run riot for the slaughter of so many souls."[46] He wrote a similar letter to Pope Alexander II ten years later, criticizing him for attaching anathemas to virtually all of his decrees, a practice Damian regarded as excessive.[47]

The saint's letters and treatises regarding moral reform typically followed the style established in the *Liber Gomorrhianus* and the *Liber Gratissimus*, founding arguments on Sacred

---

[45] Letter 112 in *Reindel*, vol. 3, 268. Translation mine.

[46] Letter 60 in *Reindel*, vol. 2, 203–205. Translation mine.

[47] Letter 164 in *Reindel*, vol. 4., 165–172.

Scripture, the Fathers of the Church, and canon law established by Church councils, which are adduced in detail to
support his position. Damian also made ample use of the
rhetorical skills he had learned in the best schools of Latin letters, expressing himself with graceful and intense prose that
revealed a deep passion for the moral integrity of the Church.

In addition to his shorter letters, which number over a
hundred, and his many poems, sermons, and hagiographies,
Damian wrote dozens of longer *opusculi* or "little works" on a
variety of theological topics. He wrote several lengthy treatises
on various aspects of monastic life.[48] His Letter 81 outlines
the Catholic faith in general,[49] and his Letter 91 defends the
proposition "That the Holy Spirit, without a doubt, proceeds
from both the Father and the Son,"[50] a recent point of conten-
tion with the upstart archbishop of Constantinople, Michael
Cerularius. Damian also defended the faith against the criticisms of Jews.[51] Perhaps his most controversial theological
work is his letter on the divine omnipotence,[52] which seeks to
resolve apparent paradoxes arising from the doctrine. At one
point in the letter Damian appears to claim that God has the
power to restore one's lost virginity, implying that God can

[48] E.g. *On the Canonical Hours* (Letter 17 in *Reindel*, vol. 1, 155–167),
On Contempt of the World (Letter 165 in *Reindel*, vol. 4, 173–230), *Domi-
nus Vobiscum* (Letter 28, in *Reindel*, vol. 1, 248–278), *On the Institutes of his
Congregation* (Letter 50 in *Reindel*, vol. 2, 77–131), *On the Perfection of Monks*
(Letter 153 in *Reindel*, vol. 4, 13–67), *Regarding Bishops who Recall Monks to
the World* (Letter 38 in *Reindel*, vol. 1, 347–373).

[49] Letter 81 in *Reindel*, vol. 2, 417–441.

[50] Letter 91 in *Reindel*, vol. 3, 1–13.

[51] *Disputation Against the Jews* (Letter 1 in *Reindel*, vol. 1, 63–102).

[52] *Disputation over the Question: if God is Omnipotent, How can he Make
Something that Happened, not to have Happened* (Letter 119 in *Reindel*, vol. 3,
341–384).

erase a past event, a view later rejected by Thomas Aquinas and other theologians. However, modern scholars are divided over this interpretation, some holding that he did not intend to imply that the past can be modified, but only that the moral state of virginity may be restored.[53]

The positions taken by the saint with regard to several important controversies would eventually become Catholic doctrine and Catholic law. His counsel to prohibit the entry into the priesthood of those with sodomitic tendencies was confirmed by the Sacred Congregation for Religious under Pope John XXIII in 1961,[54] and reaffirmed (after much painful experience following the lack of compliance with the directive) by the Congregation of Catholic Education with the express approval Pope Benedict XVI in 2005.[55] Damian's condemnation of the practice of absolving accomplices following sexual sin between a confessor and a penitent would be enshrined in the laws of the Church, which invalidate such confessions and excommunicate the priests who hear them.[56] His insistence on affirming the sacramental validity of the consecrations and ordinations of simoniacal bishops while condemning the perpetrators was also upheld against Humbert's rigorism and

[53] See Toivo J. Holopainen, "Peter Damian," in *The Stanford Encyclopedia of Philosophy*, Winter 2012 ed., at plato.stanford.edu.

[54] Holy See, Sacred Congregation of Religious, "Careful Selection and Training of Candidates for the States of Perfection and Sacred Orders," February 2, 1961, at EWTN, www.ewtn.com.

[55] Holy See, Congregation for Catholic Education, "Instruction Concerning the Criteria for the Discernment of Vocations with regard to Persons with Homosexual Tendencies in view of their Admission to the Seminary and to Holy Orders," November 4, 2005, at w2.vatican.va.

[56] See the *Code of Canon Law* (1983), can. 977, 1378, 1387; *Codex Iuris Canonici* (1917), can. 884; Pope Benedict XIV, Apostolic Constitution *Sacramentum Poenitentiae*, June 1, 1741, at w2.vatican.va.

was affirmed dogmatically at the Council of Trent.[57] Finally, his stalwart defense of clerical celibacy and rejection of a married priesthood was repeatedly upheld by the popes and is still affirmed in occidental canon law.[58]

Bishop and Cardinal

The effects of Leo IX's courageous leadership did not end with his death, for the pontiff had surrounded himself with virtuous and courageous cardinals who would succeed him on the papal throne. Leo's passing in 1054 was followed by a one year interregnum, and he was then succeeded by his cardinal appointee, Gebhard of Calw, who continued Leo's reforming mission during his two-year papacy as Pope Victor II. Following his death in 1057, he was succeeded by Pope Stephen X, who had been made Chancellor of the Roman church by Leo IX and cardinal by Victor II. During his brief reign of less than eight months Stephen also advanced the cause of reform of his two predecessors, appointing Peter Damian as Cardinal Bishop of Ostia, a small diocese contiguous with Rome, despite his reticence:

> As therefore the fame of his great sanctity and prudence could not any longer lie hidden, it was carried with clarity to the ears of the holy Roman Church, and because such a man was deemed to be ideal for the priesthood and wholly necessary for the work of the Church, having been taken to the supreme Pontiff (who was then Stephen IX)

[57] Sess. 7, can. 12 (D 855). See also Pope Nicholas II, Roman Council of 1060 (D 354); Lateran Council I, can. 1 (D 359).

[58] Eastern Catholic Churches, which comprise fewer than two percent of the Church's total population, may still ordain married men, although priests who are unmarried at ordination or who lose their wives after ordination may not remarry.

for the purpose of receiving the episcopal chair, he was thus compelled by the rest of the bishops and men of the Church, as well as by the Supreme Pontiff himself. However, as he was not forgetful of the peaceful solitude in which he was accustomed to pass his time in the reading of the Sacred Scriptures and in contemplation, and was exceedingly horrified at the prospect of losing that and returning to the noise of the city, he resisted their entreaties with the greatest effort.

Nonetheless, declaring that he would achieve nothing by his exhortations and pleading, they now began to threaten him with the sentence of excommunication if he obstinately continued to resist. What more? Finally the Apostolic Lord endeavored to add one more thing, which he could not at all disregard. He ordered, under the obligation of obedience to himself, that Damian comply with his brothers, peacefully accepting what was being asked of him, and immediately taking his right hand, he simultaneously endowed him with the ring and staff by which he joined to him the Church of Ostia.[59]

Damian's name was now joined to the distinguished ranks of reformers appointed to the cardinalate by Leo IX and his successors, names such as Hildebrand (the future Pope St. Gregory IV), Desiderius (abbot of Monte Cassino and the future Pope Bl. Victor III), and Humbert of Silva Candida. With Damian as the principal theorist of their movement, they would work together with other like-minded reformers to fight relentlessly against the vices of simony, lay investiture, and clerical incontinence, a battle which would result in triumph for papacy and usher in the era of ecclesiastical supremacy that would define the High Middle Ages.

[59] Lodi, *Vita*, cap. 14 (*Gaetani*, vol. 1, 10).

Almost immediately following his appointment as cardinal, Damian and his cohorts were faced with a grave crisis. Upon the death of Stephen X, the mafiosolike dynasty of the Tusculum counts struck another blow against the reformers, seeking to place their candidate, John Mincius, Cardinal Bishop of Velletri, on the papal throne as "Benedict X." After invading Rome and looting the papal treasury for money to bribe the citizens, they sought after Damian, who as Cardinal Bishop of Ostia had the traditional duty of conducting the rite of enthronement of the pope. But Peter had fled, retreating to his monastic home in Fonte Avellana, where he joined his voice to that of other cardinal bishops, denouncing the usurper as a simonist "wallowing in a filthy pool" of corruption.[60]

Hildebrand, returning from a mission on behalf of the Holy See to the Empress Agnes in Germany, arrived in Florence, denounced the false election of Mincius, and began to correspond with eminent Romans and others among the regional nobility to determine a candidate that would be acceptable both to reformers and the imperial court. He settled on the bishop of Florence, Gerard of Burgandy, who received the approval of Agnes and a promise of support from Godfrey, Duke of Lorraine-Tuscany. In December of 1058 the cardinals who had escaped from Rome met in the Italian city of Sienna and elected Gerard, who took the name of Nicholas II. With the military support of Godfrey and the imperial chancellor Wilbert, Nicholas advanced upon Rome in January and soon drove out Mincius, quashing the

[60] Letter 58 in *Reindel*, vol. 2, 193.

influence of the corrupt Italian baronage and consolidating the regime of the reformers.[61]

In the following year, Nicholas sent Damian with Anselm, Bishop of Lucca, on one of the most difficult missions of Damian's career: to enforce papal justice in the tumultuous archdiocese of Milan. There, an ecclesiastical civil war had broken out between local reformers, known as the "Patarines," and the main body of the largely corrupt clergy, which sought to defend its illicit practices of simony and concubinage. Hildebrand had already visited to address the situation during the papacy of Stephen, and now a committee of citizens was asking for a second intervention. Upon their arrival, Damian and Anselm convened a synod of the clergy to address the issue. They quickly found themselves to be in mortal danger, as raging crowds ran through the streets denouncing them, and the clergy of the city pressed upon them, denying the right of the papal delegation to judge the Milanese church. "They intended for me, as I might say, total destruction, and as has often been suggested to me by my friends, some of them were thirsting for my blood," wrote Damian to Hildebrand following the affair.[62]

Despite the danger, Damian held his ground and reminded the assembled clergy of the divine origin of the Church of Rome, established by Christ himself through the apostle Peter:

> Only he [Christ] founded the Roman Church, and established it on the rock of the faith that was just then being

---

[61] Months later, Damian would help reform the system of papal elections at the Lateran Synod of 1059, where the assembled clergy decided to strengthen the process by placing it primarily into the hands of the cardinal bishops, thus laying the foundation for the modern system of conclaves.

[62] Letter 65 in *Reindel*, vol. 2, 231. Translation mine.

born, who committed the rights of both terrestrial and celestial governance to the blessed holder of the keys of eternal life. Not, therefore, any earthly declaration, but that Word, by which heaven and earth were constructed, by which all of the elements were established, founded the Roman Church. It is certain that it acts by his privilege, and it is supported by his authority. There is no doubt that whoever deprives a church of its rights commits an injustice, but he who seeks to take away the privilege bestowed on the Roman Church that makes it the supreme head of all of the churches without a doubt falls into heresy, and while the first will be known as unjust, the second will be called a heretic.[63]

Peter's words succeeded in pacifying the mob of clergy and laity, an outcome that convinced Damian of the importance of emphasizing the prerogatives of the Church of Rome in the battle against corruption. After discovering that virtually all of the Milanese clergy had been ordained through simony, he decreed penances of five to seven years of periodic fasting, praying the psalms, and feeding the poor, and required that only those who were "literate, chaste, and morally distinguished"[64] be allowed to return to their clerical duties. The archbishop prostrated himself on the floor before Peter and Anselm, confessing his failure to extirpate clerical vice from his diocese, and declared his intention of traveling as a pilgrim to the tomb of St. James the Apostle in Spain as an act of penance.[65]

---

[63] Ibid., 233–234. Translation mine. Part of this statement was used later in Damian's *Disceptatio Synodalis* written for the Augsburg Synod of October 1062 (see below).

[64] Ibid., 246. Translation mine.

[65] Sadly, the reconciliation of Milan would not endure. Several years later the archbishop reneged on his promises and the conflict resumed.

Damian's skills were once more employed in the defense of the papacy when, following the death of Pope Nicholas II in 1061, the anti-reform party struck again. Damian's companion during his mission to Milan, Anselm of Lucca, was elected by the cardinals and took the name of Alexander II. Although Nicholas had established the right of the cardinal bishops to choose the pope at the Lateran Synod of 1059, requiring only the confirmation of the German emperor, the Empress Agnes would not accept this limitation of imperial power and sought to impose her own candidate upon the papacy. Refusing to receive the delegates from Rome, she organized a synod in the city of Basle with disgruntled nobles and clergy opposed to the reform party, where they elected Cadalous, the unscrupulous bishop of Parma, as pope. In the spring of 1062, styling himself as "Honorius II," Cadalous and his troops marched upon Rome to force the issue but were repulsed by the forces of Godfrey, Duke of Tuscany, who required both Cadalous and Alexander to retire until the matter could be resolved through an extraordinary synod, which was held at Augsburg in October of the same year.

While Hildebrand organized the political and military forces of the peninsula against the antipope, Damian took up his pen in defense of the papacy. He sent two scathing letters to Cadalous in mid-1062 reminding him of the Church's law regarding papal elections and citing the Scriptures and Church Fathers to urge him to relent. He also defended the election of Alexander by the cardinals in his *Disceptatio Synodalis*, an imaginary dialogue which presents the arguments for both sides in the debate, and which appears to have been directed to the Augsburg synod.[66]

[66] Patricia Ranft, *The Theology of Peter Damian* (Washington: Catholic University of America Press, 2012), 132.

Cadalous ignored Damian's entreaties and continued to plot to seize the papal throne, provoking Damian to denounce him as "that disturber of the holy Church, that overthrower of apostolic teaching, that enemy of the salvation of man, that root of sin, that herald of the devil, that apostle of the antichrist."[67] The synod decided provisionally for Alexander and ordered that an imperial delegate be sent to Rome to investigate. Following a positive report, Duke Godfrey escorted Alexander back to Rome in early 1063, where he held a synod in April excommunicating Cadalous. The pretender responded with his own synod and excommunication of Alexander, and managed to seize control of Castel Sant'Angelo, where he was besieged until he relented and fled in 1064. However, many of the bishops and noblemen opposed to clerical reform continued to submit to Cadalous, regarding him as the true pope.

While visiting France in 1063, Damian sought to finally resolve the dispute by writing to Archbishop Anno of Cologne, who had become the regent of the young emperor Henry IV, asking him to convene a general council for the purpose of confirming Alexander's pontificate.[68] Anno agreed, and the synod was held in Mantua on Pentecost of 1064, attended by Alexander, who humbly but firmly defended the validity of his election. The synod anathematized Cadalous and effectively brought his influence to an end, although the bishop of Damian's hometown, Ravenna, would continue to support Cadalous until his death.

[67] Letter 99 in *Reindel*, vol. 3, 99. See also Letter 89, in *Reindel*, vol. 2, 531–540.

[68] Pope Alexander, and particularly Hildebrand, were initially angry with Damian over his intervention because of an apparent misunderstanding over what he had written to Bishop Anno, a misunderstanding he sought to clear up by sending them a copy of the original letter. See Damian's Letter 107 in *Reindel*, vol. 3, 185–188.

As Bishop of Ostia, Peter strove to exemplify the virtues that he had long demanded of other prelates, mindful always of the accounting he would make to God for the spiritual well-being of his flock. John of Lodi tells us that Damian was careful to take advantage of the opportunity of preaching the gospel to any gathering of people, rising well before dawn in order to arrive on time. Even when ill with a fever he would arise at daybreak on Sunday to celebrate Mass and preach in a loud voice until noon, a feat that so impressed Lodi and others that they attributed it to supernatural grace. At his urging the people of the region crowded into churches to participate in the chanting of psalms during the divine office; among them were many repentant priests who had abandoned their rule of life in favor of illicit marriages.[69]

In addition to his fervent preaching, Damian busied himself with frequent visits to the sick and the poor, washing their feet in imitation of Christ and aiding them with gifts of food and clothing. The needy would throng to his home as well, where he would treat them as honored guests and feed them from his table. He frequently exhorted his clergy to imitate his practices, noting that the funds of the Church belong to all of its members. The income of priests, according to Damian,

> is sacred, and is the wage of sinners. One must beware, therefore, lest avarice or any negligent carelessness take away from the poor of Christ, to whom all of our surplus is owed in its entirety. As we have the resources available to us to give relief to the poor, diligently inquire with pious consideration to discover those nearby who are sick, or hungry, or suffer any sort of anguish of need, because by ministering the necessities of life with such

[69] Lodi, *Vita,* cap. 15 (*Gaetani,* vol. 1, 10).

pious compassion you will acquire for us and for you the common fruit of eternal reward in heaven.[70]

John of Lodi reports that, in order to find spiritual refreshment and "shake off the dust" accumulated in his worldly duties, Damian would periodically return to the hermitage of Fonte Avellana, where he would resume his penitential exercises and accuse himself of sin before his brothers during chapter meetings, in accordance with the monastic rule.[71] He longed to stay and asked the pope to accept his resignation, writing long letters both to the pontiff and to Hildebrand vindicating the right of bishops to renounce their positions.[72] It is not clear when or if he was ultimately relieved of his see by the pope; assuming that he was, the date could be as early as 1063 and as late as 1070.[73]

---

[70] Lodi, *Vita*, cap. 17 (*Gaetani*, vol. 1, 12). Translation mine.

[71] Ibid., cap. 18 (*Gaetani*, vol. 1, 13).

[72] That is, Letters 57 and 72 in *Reindel*, vol. 2.

[73] Historians differ on this question, which may be impossible to resolve with certainty. Owen Blum favors the date of 1063 for Damian's retirement in his book *St. Peter Damian: His Teaching on the Spiritual Life* (Washington: Catholic University of America Press, 1947), 35, note 138, but a letter dated by Reindel to 1070 (Letter 169 in *Reindel*, vol. 4, 247–249) refers to his resignation as if it had not yet happened. Damian's Letter 96, which Reindel assigns to the year 1063, indicates that in some way he had been relieved of his pontifical duties (see *Reindel*, vol. 3, 46–47). The French historian Reginald Biron concludes that Damian's retirement is announced in his letter 57, which is dated by Reindel to 1058, in *St. Pierre Damien (1007–1072)*, 20th ed. (Paris: Lecoffre, 1908), 164. However, Damian's principal modern biographer, Jean Leclerq, in his *Saint Pierre Damien, ermite et homme d'eglise* (Rome : Edizioni di storia e letteratura, 1960), 111, concludes that Damian continued in his position as Cardinal Bishop of Ostia after 1063 but had permission to live at Fonte Avellana due to health concerns, and ceased to be bishop in 1067.

Emissary and Reformer

Damian lost no momentum in his relentless drive for ecclesiastical reform during the last decade of his life. In addition to his occasional duties as papal legate, he maintained a continuous correspondence with the pope, cardinals, bishops, fellow priests and monks, secular rulers, relatives, and others, which often took the form of short treatises on a variety of important topics. His missions on behalf of the pope took him by precarious routes to France and Germany, where he did battle against clerical vices and defended the sanctity of marriage against the emperor himself. So great was his importance to Pope Alexander II that he declared that, after himself, Damian was "the highest authority within the Roman Church," and said of him that he was "like our eye and the unwavering support of the Apostolic See."[74]

At the Roman synod in April of 1063, abbot Hughes of Cluny had arrived to report that his abbey had been attacked by the forces of Bishop Drogon of the local diocese of Macon, which were seeking to usurp the traditional independence of Cluny, long conceded to it by the popes. He asked for an embassy of the Roman Church to be sent to correct the misbehavior of Drogon and his allies and to vindicate the rights of Cluny, which was the most important monastic institution in Europe, ruling over a vast number of monasteries throughout the continent.

When others present at the synod demurred out of fear of the violence of Drogon, the aging Damian offered himself for the perilous and lengthy mission, and Alexander II accepted the offer. Despite the danger of attack by the partisans

---

[74] *Diploma de Legatione S. Petri Damiani in Gallias* (PL 145, 857B).

of Cadalous and the difficult weather, Damian set out with Hughes and his small entourage, navigating through the snowy Alps on horseback, all the while insisting on maintaining his fasts and penitential exercises. Accompanying him was a letter from the pope to local bishops declaring, "We have given to him (Peter Damian) our authority so that everything he will decree in your provinces, by the aid of God, will be held to be ratified and confirmed as if we had promulgated it by our own particular judgment."[75]

Upon his arrival, Damian found himself addressing a related emergency. The monks of Saint-Martial, a monastery recently placed under the authority of Cluny following decades of corruption, had revolted following the death of their prior and had assaulted the monks sent by Hughes to arrange the monastery's affairs. Damian traveled several hundred kilometers to Saint-Martial to confront the monks, who hid from him and refused to present themselves to make their case. After entreating them several times to come forth, Damian declared their excommunication in the diocesan cathedral, to the delight of the crowd assembled there. The corrupt monks vacated the property and were replaced by Clunaic brothers, who went on to revitalize the monastery in the years that followed.

Damian then returned to confront Drogon and his allies, whose violent usurpations he met with calm resolution and superior organization. Avoiding a direct clash between himself and the bishop, Damian called a regional council of bishops to discuss the legal status of Cluny. There, before Drogon and all of the assembled episcopacy, he ordered to be read

---

[75] *Diploma de Legatione* (PL 145, 857B–858B). An ancient account of Damian's journey can be found in *De Gallica Profectione Domini Petri Damiani* (PL 145, 865–880).

aloud the original papal decree granting Cluny's independence from the local bishop and establishing its direct accountability to the pope, a decree whose authenticity none could deny. Drogon quickly capitulated and reconciled with Hughes and his monks. The day had been won peacefully and decisively, and Damian's example of holiness was never forgotten by the monks of Cluny, who promised to offer Mass for his soul every year and were among the first to celebrate his feast day following his death.

Damian showed similar courage in his embassy to the city of Florence in 1067, although the outcome was not so satisfactory. The city's bishop, Peter, had been accused of simony by groups of monks and laity, who were consequently refusing the sacraments from the clergy he had ordained. Sent by Pope Alexander to address the charges and resolve the dispute, Damian was confronted by unruly and violent mobs who would not listen to reason. He pointed out that he himself could not make a judgment regarding the accusation of simony and that the citizens could have recourse to Rome's upcoming annual synod of bishops to present their case. Moreover, he observed, the sacraments remained valid despite any simony on the part of the city's bishop or clergy, and yet many of the faithful were dying without the last rites for fear of their invalidity. His remonstrances fell upon deaf ears, and he was forced to return from his mission without having resolved the matter.[76] Although the bishop's opponents followed Damian's advice and brought their case to Alexander at the following Roman synod, the pope also found the crisis

---

[76] The full account of the event is found in a letter written by Damian to the citizens and monks of Florence, dated to 1067 by Reindel. See Letter 146 in *Reindel*, vol. 3, 531–542.

difficult to address, and due to a lack of sufficient evidence against the bishop, repeatedly refused to rule against him.

Two years later, Damian was sent by Pope Alexander to Germany to defend the sacrament of marriage against the German emperor Henry IV, a young man notorious for his lechery and marital infidelity.[77] Henry had become estranged from his wife, Bertha, and had sought a divorce from Siegfried, Archbishop of Mainz, at the Synod of Worms in 1069, claiming that the marriage had never been consummated and that the two were incompatible. Although the bishops in attendance at the synod would later reveal their opposition to the plan, none showed the courage to defy the emperor to his face, and they agreed to settle the matter at a council to be held in late September in the city of Mainz. Siegfried then sought the advice of Pope Alexander II, who decided to send Peter Damian to represent him before the emperor and reject his illegitimate divorce.[78]

When Henry heard that Damian had arrived in Mainz to issue judgment against him, he fled to Frankfurt and attempted to reconvene his nobles and bishops there. However, Damian would not be refused. He followed the emperor to Frankfurt, and before the assembled crowd he announced the pope's decision. According to the account of contemporary historian Lambert of Hersfeld, Damian told the emperor that

> what he intended to do was most evil, and even more abhorrent in that it would be in the name of a Christian, and even a king. If he were not so much terrified by the laws of man or the sanctions of ecclesiastical law, he should spare at least his reputation and good name, lest the poison of such an indecent example, taken at first by the king,

[77] See Bruno of Merseberg, *De Bello Saxonico* (Hannover, 1880), 5.

[78] Biron, *St. Pierre Damien*, 178–180.

contaminate the whole Christian people, and he who had had the role of avenging crimes become the author and standard-bearer of such scandal. Finally, if he did not bow to these counsels, it would be necessary for the pope to apply ecclesiastical force and to prohibit this sin by means of canon law, and his hands would never consecrate an emperor who would betray the Christian faith with such a pestilent example.[79]

Lambert reports that, upon hearing Damian's words, "all the princes who were present rose up" against Henry and "expressed their agreement with the Roman pontiff, and beseeched God that no sin might be inflicted against His glory and that the majesty of the royal name might not be contaminated by the filth of such an indecent act."[80] The emperor quickly capitulated, agreeing to remain in his marriage, and Bertha was soon pregnant. Damian's courage, backed by the resolve of Alexander II, had again won the day.

Death and Canonization

In early 1072, Pope Alexander sent Peter on his final mission: to reconcile his home town of Ravenna following the death of its schismatic bishop Henry, who had clung to the antipope Cadalous and had been excommunicated with his entire diocese by Alexander.[81] Although Damian's health was failing, John of Lodi tells us that he rejoiced at the opportunity to reconcile the city of his birth with the Catholic Church, and

[79] Lambertus Hersfeldensis, *Annales*, 2nd ed. (Hannover, 1874), 76. Translation mine.

[80] Ibid. Translation mine.

[81] Peter had previously written to Alexander asking him to lift the excommunication against Henry, perhaps because the latter had repented before his death. See Letter 167 in *Reindel*, vol. 4, p 237.

in some way repay the debt he felt he owed to the city from which he had received so many benefits in his youth.[82]

Although the bishop had "miserably polluted the people" of Ravenna by his bad example and had "profaned the whole church with his unlawful audacities," the city was awed and grateful to receive a son who had become so famous for his sanctity, learning, and leadership, according to John of Lodi. Peter was "received into the hands of the citizens with immense joy." "Exceedingly delighted" by the saint, and "giving great thanks to God for caring for them and to the vicar of Christ for having sent such a man to them," they "humbly did penance for their offense." Damian then gave them the papal absolution, and "throughout the city there was a great exulting."[83]

On his journey back from Ravenna, Peter and his entourage stopped at Faenza, where Damian had gone to school as a youth, to stay the night in the monastery of Santa Maria degli Angeli. There Damian was seized by a fever and was confined to his bed for eight days. In the deep of night on the eve or early morning of the feast of the Chair of St. Peter at Antioch (February 22), he commanded his monks to pray the office of Matins with him, "wishing first to carry out the rites of the apostolic solemnity, and thus finally to leave in security."[84] Shortly after the completion of the office, he passed away.

Upon learning of his death, the population of Faenza immediately began to crowd into the monastery, jostling with one another for the chance to kiss and touch the body of the saint or his shroud, and preventing Damian's brothers from carrying his body away. He was entombed in the monastery

---

[82] Lodi, *Vita,* cap. 21 (*Gaetani*, vol. 1, 15).

[83] Ibid. Translation mine.

[84] Ibid., cap. 22. Translation mine.

chapel in a white sarcophagus near the entrance to the choir, and the monks began to celebrate the office and festive mass of his "heavenly birth" on February 23. Peter's informal canonization continued as his feast spread to Monte Cassino, Cluny, and Ravenna and its suffragan dioceses. His body was later transferred to a Jesuit church, then to the diocesan cathedral in 1825. In 1898 a special chapel was attached to the cathedral to house his remains.

In 1823, Pope Leo XII confirmed the prophesy of his eleventh century namesake, who had assured Damian that he would someday "rejoice in the celestial mansion with the Son of God and of the Virgin," by adding Damian's feast to the universal calendar and awarding him the title "Doctor of the Catholic Church."

TRANSLATOR'S PREFACE

The *Liber Gomorrhianus* or "Book of Gomorrah"[1] occupies a singular place in the literature of the Catholic Church. It is undoubtedly the most stirringly eloquent and impassioned denunciation of sexual perversion ever penned by a Catholic saint, and carries a soaring and unreserved endorsement by a saint-pope who virtually canonizes him while still alive. Although it was written almost a thousand years ago, the *Book of Gomorrah* in many ways seems addressed to our own times, associating the phenomena of clerical homosexual behavior and pederasty, and endorsing the imprisonment of clergy who are a danger to youth. It expresses an unremitting hatred for the sin of sodomy and simultaneously a deep compassion for its perpetrators, seeking their reconciliation with God and assuring them of hope for salvation. It also acknowledges the threat of an ecclesiastical establishment seeking to turn a blind eye to the problem of clerical corruption and to conceal its sins, rather than rooting out the problem.

---

[1] This title has been used to refer to the book since the 14th century, but seems not to have been used by Peter Damian nor his contemporaries. This has led Glenn W. Olsen, an important Damian scholar, in his *Sodomites, Effeminates, Hermaphrodites, and Androgynes* (Toronto: Pontifical Institute for Medieval Studies, 2011), 203, 209, to criticize those who use this ancient title and to propose as an alternative the even less historical "Letter 31," taken from the numbering system used by Kurt Reindel in his critical edition of Damian's letters. However, I have opted to retain the traditional title, which has been given to the work by a long-standing consensus within the Catholic Church, even if it does not originate with Damian himself.

The author of this great work, St. Peter Damian, was an Italian eremitic monk and future Doctor of the Church who lead a family of monasteries based at Fonte Avellana, the members of which were devoted to the strictest ascetic practices. He addressed his *opusculum* or "little work" to Leo IX (1049–54), one of a handful of popes from the second millennium who would be canonized as a saint. Both Leo and Damian were impassioned reformers, comrades-in-arms, fighting not against external threats, but against the enervating effects of moral laxity and corruption within the Church itself. The *Book of Gomorrah* would be one of many *opusculi* and letters Damian would write against the misbehavior of monks and clergymen, behavior that included sexual immorality of every kind, as well as the practice of simony; that is, the purchasing of clerical ordination.

The effect of Damian's arguments, which are bolstered by copious references to the Scriptures, the Fathers of the Church, and traditional canon law, is augmented by his abilities as a classically-trained Latinist who had already established his fame as a teacher of rhetoric following his formal training in the best schools of Italy. Although his style is sometimes strained and labored, Damian's prose often soars in its cadence and its use of metaphor, and he is able to draw upon a vast repertoire of adjectives and literary allusions from both sacred and profane literature. His mastery of the language's grammar and literary forms rank him among the greatest Latinists of the Middle Ages.[2]

The relevance of the *Book of Gomorrah* for the modern Church is immediately recognizable to anyone even remotely

---

[2] Jean Leclercq, *Pierre Damien, ermite et homme d'Église* (Rome: Edizioni di storia e letteratura, 1960), 172, cited by Pope Benedict XVI, General Audience, Paul VI Audience Hall, September 9, 2009, at w2.vatican.va.

aware of the compromised reputation of the Catholic clergy
throughout the modern West, a situation that has arisen in
large part due to an increasingly effeminate priesthood and a
lax or indifferent view of sodomy and sexual immorality that
seems to reach to the highest levels of the Catholic hierarchy.
It was precisely such attitudes that Peter Damian was seeking
to combat in the eleventh century by urging the restoration of
the Church's strong penitential canons relating to sodomy and
the permanent suspension of clergymen who were habitually
inclined to such behavior. There is particularly bitter irony
for the modern reader in Damian's citation of traditional laws
that rigorously punish child sex abusers, sending them to monastic prisons for the rest of their lives for a single offense. In
the *Book of Gomorrah* we hear the voice of a prophet speaking
to us over the span of centuries, reminding us of vital truths
we have abandoned, and calling us to repentance.

Structure and Themes of the Book of Gomorrah

As the traditional title of Damian's work would suggest, the
central topic of the *Book of Gomorrah* is the vice of "sodomy."
This expression derives from the name of one of two cities
destroyed by God in the book of Genesis,[3] the city of Sodom,
which is condemned to fiery obliteration for the practice of
homosexuality,[4] while Damian's work is named after the second of the two cities, Gomorrah, which met the same fate.

---

[3] Genesis 19.

[4] Although other reasons are also given in the Old Testament for the
destruction of the cities of Sodom and Gomorrah (such as neglect of
the poor, and arrogance; see Ezek. 16:49–50), both the Old and New
Testaments clearly associate sexual immorality and perversion with the
condemnation of the two cities (see Gen. 19:4–9; Ezek.16:50; Jer. 23:14;
Jude 7).

It is significant that Damian's denunciation of this sin, one he regards as widespread among the clergy of his day, employs a definition of the term that is broader than modern usage would suggest. Damian sees "sodomy" as comprising all unnatural sexual practices, making anal intercourse the most egregious of a range of acts that contradict the natural purpose of human sexuality. For Damian, therefore, "sodomy" is used to refer to the following practices in decreasing order of moral gravity: homosexual anal copulation, homosexual femoral copulation, mutual masturbation, and solitary masturbation, to which list contraception and bestiality are added as species of the same sin.[5] Catholic doctrine holds that all of these practices deviate in varying degrees from the natural purpose of human sexuality, which exists to consummate an exclusive and perpetual union of a man and a woman ordered to the procreation of offspring; as such they are regarded as gravely immoral.[6] Damian's descriptions of these sins, although not gratuitously graphic, are specific and clear, and were so explicit by the standards of the early seventeenth century, when Damian's complete works were first printed, that its editors felt compelled to delete, expurgate, or paraphrase several paragraphs of the work, particularly in chapters 3, 7, and 23, as well as Pope Leo's own letter to Damian in response. Even with these modifications, later

---

[5] Damian initially establishes four grades of sodomy in chapter two, which are (in decreasing order of severity): anal copulation, femoral copulation, mutual masturbation, and solitary masturbation. In chapter fourteen he shows that sodomy is comparable to bestiality in historic canon law. In chapter four he makes contraception, specifically the sin of Onan (who withdrew at the moment of ejaculation; see Genesis 38:9–10) a species of sodomy as well. However, he does not indicate the place of bestiality and contraception within his system of gradation.

[6] See the *Catechism of the Catholic Church*, par. 2357.

commentators warned about the danger to young minds posed by the text.[7] However, such precise language regarding immoral sexual behavior was standard fare during the tenth and eleventh centuries, particularly in penitential manuals from the period which seek to establish clear definitions of different categories of offense.[8]

Moral Laxity and False Mercy

Damian is confronting a culture of clerical corruption and moral indifference among many in the eleventh century Church, a mindset that often ignored or minimized Christian theological and legal traditions regarding immoral sexual behavior. The situation was symptomatic of the general and catastrophic social decline brought about during the *saecula obscura* of the ninth and tenth centuries, which had only recently abated. Damian's task is to reassert the Catholic Church's doctrine regarding unnatural sexual acts and the traditional penances prescribed for them in the Church's canon law ordained during the earliest centuries of Christianity.

Damian begins in chapter one by summarizing the problem for Pope Leo, warning that the vice of sodomy is spreading among monks and clerics and that it must be quashed immediately while it is still possible to do so. After enumerating the grades of sodomy in chapter two, he proceeds in chapter three to address the problem as a crisis of authority in the

---

[7] See Reginald Biron, *St. Pierre Damien (1007–1072)*, 20th ed. (Paris: Victor Lecoffre, 1908), 56–57.

[8] E.g. the *Corrector*, the nineteenth book of Burchard of Worms's *Libri Decretorum* (PL 140, 949A–1014C), an eleventh-century work which is believed to supply much of the source material for Damian's chapters on faulty canonical manuals, has similarly detailed descriptions of sexual sins.

Church, noting that many prelates are permitting practicing homosexuals to continue functioning as priests, despite having knowledge of their misdeeds. He regards this as an "impious" and "excessive" form of mercy that leads to even worse corruption. This false mercy, which he also characterizes as "cruel" in chapter 12, will be contrasted in later chapters with the authentic mercy of God, which is always offered to those who repent of even the worst of sins.

In chapters 4–6, he argues that permitting such clerics to continue performing the sacrifice of the Mass, even in cases of priest shortages, is contrary to Scripture, the Church Fathers, and reason itself. He also decries those who seek after the order of the priesthood or continue in the priesthood after having fallen into sodomitic vices. He then proceeds (in chapters 7–10) to analyze the aggravating circumstances that worsen the sin of sodomy, particularly the sexual abuse of "spiritual sons" (penitents) by confessors, and the mutual absolution of accomplices through the exchange of sacramental confession.

Damian's thundering invective in these early chapters is suffused with quotations and citations of Sacred Scripture, which is Damian's primary source and inspiration throughout the work. He invokes Genesis 19 to demonstrate that sodomy is the worst of sins, noting that "when he [God] had not yet placed a legal precept prohibiting it along with the other vices, he was already condemning it with the censure of strict retribution—not to mention that he destroyed Sodom and Gomorrah,[9] which were two distinguished cities, and all the neighboring regions, with sulfur and fire sent from heaven." He adds the punishment of Onan in Genesis 38 as another proof of the spiritually deadly nature of sodomy, as well as the law of Moses in Leviticus 20. These examples

[9] See Gen. 19.

are bolstered by citations of the New Testament, such as 1 Timothy 1 and Romans 1, which Damian uses to reinforce his argument that those who have fallen into sodomy should not seek ordination.

The Historical and Legal Case for Punishing Sexual Perversion

In chapters 11–15 Damian proceeds to establish a legal case regarding the punishment of sodomy among the clergy. This requires him to enter into a long digression on Church law in which he argues for the falsity of weaker canons that are found listed in many contemporary reference works (chapters 11–13). His claim that the penitential manuals contained inaccuracies was not a novel one; such manuals had been repeatedly condemned for their errors in previous centuries, in particular with regard to lax penances assigned to homosexual acts.[10] Damian then launches into a series of *a fortiori* arguments in favor of stronger penalties for clergy by reference to the canons of the Council of Ancyra, held in 314 A.D. (chapters 14–15). Such precise and fixed penances were gradually fading from the Church's custom and would ultimately be abandoned in favor of the individual judgment of confessors, and Damian himself does not insist that they be applied in their full rigor (as he makes explicit in chapter 25). However, as he makes clear in later passages of the work, his purpose is not to insist on a particular penalty for sodomy,

---

[10] For example, by the Council of Chalons in 814 (see *Mansi*, vol. 14, 101), which complains in canon 38 that penitential books have "certain errors" and "uncertain authors" and mandates the "repudiation" and "elimination" of such books.

but rather to demonstrate the gravity of the sin and the need to root it out from the clergy.

Damian's second major source (in chapter 16) is a monastic law penalizing child sexual abuse which was written by St. Fructuosus of Braga (d. 665), a Spanish abbot and monastic reformer. This canon found its way into other collections of ecclesiastical law during the early Middle Ages, where it began to be falsely attributed to St. Basil. The contrast it presents between the recent scandalous leniency regarding pedophile priests on the part of many Catholic bishops and the firm approach of medieval canonists, is striking. According to the canon, those monks who are guilty of lascivious contact of any kind with children or adolescents are to be publicly humiliated, confined for a year in a monastic cell subject to heavy penances, and are to remain under the guard of two other monks, presumably in perpetuity. In the same chapter Damian also cites a decree of Pope St. Siricius (384–99) prohibiting priests to remain in holy orders and prohibiting laymen to receive holy orders if they have committed an offense requiring a canonical penance.

Damian's extensive critique of what he regards as faulty reference works circulating among the monasteries, which he attributes to willful acts of subversion by interested parties, is evidence of a broader problem brought on by the turbulence of the tenth century: the proliferation of hastily copied manuscripts of questionable accuracy. Such manuscripts were often plagued by faulty or paraphrased quotations, erroneous attributions or plagiarized texts lacking any attribution, and insertions and deletions by copyists. As I observe below, these problems affected Damian's own trusted sources, leading to erroneous attributions of several of his most important quotations. Nonetheless, the texts quoted by Damian all originated with Church Fathers, early ecclesiastical writers, or saints, and therefore retain their weight in the context of the argument.

The Spiritual and Psychological Destructiveness of Sodomy

After making the doctrinal and legal case for the punishment of sexual perversion, Damian now launches his own extended assault upon the vice of sodomy itself (chapters 17–19), bringing to bear his formidable Latinity in the service of his cause. He describes in harrowing detail the terrible effects of such behavior on its practitioners, who are devastated spiritually and psychologically. Although his hatred of sexual perversion is intense, it is directed not to the person but to the sin, and Damian expresses an equally intense compassion for those who are caught in its snare, mourning "the noble soul, made in the image and likeness of God, and united with the most precious blood of Christ, more glorious than many buildings, certainly to be preferred to all the pinnacles of earthly workmanship" and lamenting "the fall of the eminent soul, and the destruction of the temple in which Christ had dwelt."

It should be noted that, while Damian condemns homosexual acts repeatedly, he does not identify them with what is today understood as a homosexual "orientation"—the notion that same-sex attraction may be deeply embedded in the psychology of homosexual actors. Damian's work, therefore, is not a criticism of those who merely suffer from homosexual urges or temptations, but rather those who act upon them. However, in chapter 18 Damian seeks to analyze the implicit motives of those who engage in same-sex sodomy, accusing them of denying their own masculinity and of seeking a false complementarity in others of their own gender:

> Speak O emasculated man! Respond O effeminate man!
> What do you seek in a man that you are unable to find in
> yourself—what difference of sexes, what diverse features
> of members, what softness, what tenderness of carnal al-
> lurement, what pleasantness of a smooth face? The vigor
> of masculine appearance should frighten you, I entreat
> you, and your mind should abhor virile limbs. The pur-
> pose of the natural appetite is that each one seek externally
> what he is not able to find within the enclosure of his
> own means. If, therefore, the handling of masculine flesh
> delights you, turn your hands to yourself, and know that
> whatever you do not find in yourself, you seek in vain in
> another body.

The latter part of chapter 19, as well as all of chapters 20–22, are dedicated to Damian's argument that it is inappropriate for those who are habituated to the sin of sodomy to carry out priestly functions; that is, to offer the sacrifice of the Mass, hear confessions, and carry out the other sacraments of the Catholic Church. Damian is not here arguing, as is sometimes claimed, that the sacraments are invalidated by the sins of the priest, but rather that such priests are guilty of sacrilege, provoke the wrath of God, and subvert the morality of the faithful. Damian's acknowledgment of the validity of sacra-ments performed by unworthy ministers is evidenced by his *Liber Gratissimus*, written around the same time, in which he defends the sacramental validity of ordinations of priests by simoniacal bishops.

After reiterating in chapter 23 that even the lowest de-gree of sodomy (that is, solitary masturbation) is a grave sin, Damian offers words of encouragement to those who have fallen into such vices (chapters 24–25), expressing great com-passion for their plight, and reminding them that they should "beware, lest the abyss of despair swallow you up" and instead "faithfully trust in divine kindness." He counsels those who are habituated to unnatural sexual practices to meditate on the glory in heaven that awaits them if they repent, and on the torments of hell if they do not. He also recommends the use of fasting and other penitential measures to subdue the stubborn "ass" of the flesh and subject it to the soul.

The Responsibility of Prelates for the Sins of Their Subjects

In chapter 26, Damian defends his authorship of the *Liber Gomorrhianus* from detractors who feel scandalized by his criticisms and regard him as having betrayed the clergy by exposing their sins. He uses the opportunity to remind his readers of their own grave obligation to correct evils of which they are aware, and of the divine punishments promised in the Scriptures to those who fail to do so. To this end, he invokes the examples of the Church Fathers, such as Ambrose and Jerome, who rebuked the evils of heresy and schism with similar vigor. He clarifies that he is not seeking to incite hatred against anyone, but rather to bring about their salvation by denouncing the sin that harms them, a theme that is familiar to Christians of all stripes who today battle against the social and legal acceptance of sodomy.

Finally, in chapter 27, Damian asks Leo to respond to him with instructions for addressing such sins, which would have been applicable to his own community of hermitages and presumably throughout the Church. Although he had sought at length in chapters 11–16 to establish that traditional ecclesiastical law required the degradation of all clerics guilty in any way of sodomy, he suggests here a graded system of punishment that would allow those whose offenses are less severe and involve fewer accomplices to return to the clerical state following the completion of their penance, while permanently barring from clerical office those who are guilty of worst grades of offense or who have participated with large numbers of accomplices. In deference to the authority of the pope, he asks him to make the final determination on the matter.

In his letter of response, Leo praises Damian in the highest terms and accepts his suggested system of penalties, decreeing that those who are guilty of the lower three degrees of offense in Damian's scheme (masturbation, mutual masturbation, and femoral copulation) and with few partners, should be restored to the clerical state after a suitable penance. However, to this he adds another condition: that the offense must have been infrequent. Those guilty of anal copulation even once, or of frequent participation in the lower degrees, or of having committed such sins with a large number of partners, were to be prohibited from reentering the clerical state. Leo's system of penalties, therefore, is somewhat more severe than that which Damian has recommended, adding the frequency of commission as a criterion for excluding clerics from their office.

The Rejection Thesis and Other Misinterpretations of the Book of Gomorrah

During the course of the twentieth century, a form of revisionist scholarship has been applied to the *Liber Gomorrhianus* which tends to vitiate its reputation as an exemplar of Catholic doctrine or to reinterpret it in ways that serve agendas that are alien or even opposed to Damian's purposes. Principal among these is what I will call the "rejection thesis," the claim that Damian's work was downplayed, ignored, and even rejected by Pope St. Leo IX. The rejection thesis holds, according to one narrative, that Leo received the book with little enthusiasm and even coolness or rebuke, rejecting Damian's recommendations for penal sanctions against clerics guilty of sodomy in favor of more lenient measures. In other versions it is asserted that Leo was at first pleased with the work but was then persuaded that it was exaggerated, and turned a cold shoulder to Damian. Some authors have even claimed that Leo was positively unconcerned with the problem of clerical sodomy, regarding it as a trifling matter. Finally, at least one recent commentator claims that Pope Alexander II removed the *Book of Gomorrah* from Damian's possession.

Although elements of the rejection thesis may be found in earlier historical accounts of Damian's life, it seems first to have appeared in its completed and explicit form in the early years of the 20th century, beginning with Horace K. Mann's *The Lives of the Popes in the Middle Ages* (1910).[11] Mann's novel interpretation, in various forms, then appeared in volume eleven of *The Catholic Encyclopedia* (1911),[12] and volume four of the *Dictionnaire de Theologie Catholique* (1939).[13] It was then repeated in a variety of works, including those of revisionist scholars seeking to undermine the traditional Christian

[11] Horace K. Mann, *The Lives of the Popes in the Middle Ages*, vol. 6 (St. Louis: B. Herder, 1910).

[12] Leslie Alexander St. Lawrence Toke, "Peter Damian," in *The Catholic Encyclopedia*, vol. 11, 764–766 (New York: Robert Appleton Company, 1911). Toke does not cite Mann's work in his bibliography, but Mann was also a contributor to the eleventh volume and given that Mann appears to be the first to advance the rejection thesis, it seems probable that his work (or his personal influence) was the source of the same thesis appearing in Toke's entry.

[13] Georges Bareille, "DAMIEN (Saint Pierre)," In *Dictionnaire de Theologie Catholique*, vol. 4, 40–54 (Paris: Librairie Letouzey et Ane, 1939).

condemnation of sodomy, such as Derrick Bailey's *Homosexuality and the Western Christian Tradition* (1955)[14] and John Boswell's *Christianity, Social Tolerance, and Homosexuality* (1982),[15] and continues to appear in the academic literature on Damian, with little justification to support it.

Mann's version of the thesis claims that Leo expressed a vague acceptance of the *Liber Gomorrhianus*, but rejected Damian's recommendations for penalizing the offense. "Hence, so far from approving of the drastic measures proposed by St. Peter, he would not *(nos humanius agentes)* even go so far as strict justice and canon law exacted, but would only decree deposition against those clerks who were guilty of the most criminal offences," writes Mann.[16] Moreover, Mann adds, a backlash was provoked among those scandalized by the accusations or stung by the criticism and "these views were duly impressed upon the Pope" who, fearing that "he had an ally whose very zeal made him dangerous ... showed himself less favourable to him."[17]

This change of attitude on the part of the pope "cut the sensitive soul of Damian," Mann claims, and Damian wrote a letter defending himself in response.[18] Mann notes that the pope's reaction to this letter is not recorded, but he quotes the French historian Delarc regarding the consequences: "It is certain that Peter Damian only played a very secondary part

[14] Derrick Sherwin Bailey, *Homosexuality and the Western Christian Tradition* (London: Longman's, Green, 1955).

[15] John Boswell, *Christianity, Social Tolerance, and Homosexuality* (Chicago: University of Chicago Press, 1980).

[16] Mann, *The Lives of the Popes*, 51. *Nos humanius agentes* ("we, acting more humanely") is a quotation of Leo's letter. See the full translation of the letter preceding my translation of the *Book of Gomorrah*.

[17] Mann, *The Lives of the Popes*, 52.

[18] That is, Letter 33, which will be addressed in detail below.

during the reign of Leo IX."[19] Mann does not provide a citation for his account regarding the reaction to the *Liber Gomorrhianus*.

Elements of Mann's rejection narrative then found their way into Catholic reference works of the period. According to Leslie Toke, writing in *The Catholic Encyclopedia* (1911): "Even the pope, who had at first praised the work, was persuaded that it was exaggerated, and his coldness drew from Damian a vigorous letter of protest."[20] A similar statement by Georges Bareille in his Peter Damian entry for the *Dictionnaire de Theologie Catholique* of 1939, which seems to be inspired by the earlier *Catholic Encyclopedia* entry, does not mention the praise heaped upon the work by Leo, but states rather that "the pontiff bears himself even somewhat coldly towards him, to which Damian reacts in a very sensitive manner."[21] A faint echo of the same claim can even be found in Owen Blum's important work *St. Peter Damian: His Teaching on the Spiritual Life* (1949), in which he states that "Leo did not take so readily to Damian's severity, yet he expressed his joy at the edification Damian gave by his life and his teachings."[22]

This narrative then found its way into the work of English-speaking scholars seeking to minimize the gravity of sodomy or even to vindicate it.[23] In his *Homosexuality and the Western*

[19] Mann, *The Lives of the Popes*, 53. For full context, see M. l'Abbe Delarc, *Un Pape Alsacien: essai historique sur Saint Léon IX et son temps* (Paris: E. Plon, 1876), 166.

[20] Toke, "Peter Damian," 765.

[21] "Le pontife lui témoigna même quelque froideur, à laquelle Damien se montra très sensible." Bareille, "DAMIEN (Saint Pierre)," 42. Translation mine.

[22] Blum, *St. Peter Damian*, 20–21.

[23] French and German scholars appear to have generally discarded the rejection thesis or seem to have been unaware of it, most notably Damian's principal modern biographer Jean Leclercq in his *Saint Pierre*

Christian Tradition (1955), revisionist theologian Derrick Bailey claims that "Leo IX himself began to have second thoughts. Further reflection ... convinced him that Peter had gone too far, and he felt bound to administer a check to the reformer's zeal. After commending, therefore, the motive behind his courageous and forthright defense of chastity and condemnation of clerical vice, the pope went on to rebuke his harsh and unyielding spirit."[24] This claim of a "rebuke" is echoed by Pierre Payer in his introduction to his translation of the *Liber Gomorrhianus*, in which he writes that Leo "not only differs from Damian but seems to issue a mild rebuke."[25]

The homosexual revisionist scholar John Boswell proceeds in the same vein in his *Christianity, Social Tolerance, and Homosexuality* (1980), claiming that "Leo declined to accede to Peter's demand that all clerics guilty of any sort of homosexual offense be removed from office and insisted, rather, that clerics who had not engaged in such activities 'as a long-standing practice or with many men' should remain in the same rank they held when convicted, and that only those in the most severely sinful states might be degraded from their rank."[26] In reference to this claim of Leo's rejection of Damian's "demand," Boswell finds it "particularly striking that Saint Leo should have disagreed with Saint Peter on this matter"[27] given

---

Damien, ermite et homme d'eglise (Rome: Edizioni di storia e letteratura, 1960), 70. Among anglophone scholars it is notably refuted by William D. McCready, *Odiosa sanctitas: St. Peter Damian, Simony, and Reform* (Toronto: Pontifical Institute of Medieval Studies, 2011), 211–215.

[24] Bailey, *Homosexuality*, 114, cited in Boswell, *Christianity*, 212.

[25] *Book of Gomorrah: An Eleventh-Century Treatise against Clerical Homosexual Practices*, ed. and trans. Pierre J. Payer (Waterloo, Ontario: Wilfrid Laurier University Press: 1982), 18.

[26] Boswell, *Christianity*, 212.

[27] Ibid.

their agreement on other points, and adds that "Peter in fact had no luck in convincing anyone that gay sexuality deserved hostile attention, although he was extremely influential in the reform movements of the day."[28] Moreover, Boswell adds, the book was seen in such a negative light that it was taken by force from Damian by Pope Alexander II, who "actually stole the Liber Gomorrhianus from Peter and kept it locked up."[29]

Boswell's embrace of the rejection thesis is uncritically accepted by Patricia Ranft in her recent work *The Theology of Peter Damian* (2012). Ranft repeats the claim that Leo "disagrees" with Damian "about disciplining the guilty," affirming that "Damian wanted clerics guilty of sodomy removed from office," while "Leo would remove only the hard-core practitioner." She also accepts Boswell's assertion that the bishops in general were unpersuaded regarding the problem, erroneously claiming that "the hierarchy did not address the problem in any councils," and approvingly quoting Boswell's claim that "Peter in fact had no luck in convincing anyone that gay sexuality deserved hostile attention."[30] Even the more nuanced Glenn Olsen, a critic of Boswell, accepts the essence of the rejection thesis in his recent work *Sodomites, Effeminates, Hermaphrodites, and Androgynes* (2011), although he seeks to defend Leo's supposed rejection of Damian's recommendations.[31]

Despite the popularity of the rejection thesis among recent scholars, it appears to be little more than an enduring scholarly

[28] Ibid., 213.

[29] Ibid.

[30] Patricia Ranft, *The Theology of Peter Damian : 'Let Your Life Always Serve As A Witness.'* (Washington, D.C.: Catholic University of America Press, 2012), 88–89.

[31] Olsen, *Sodomites*, 206–207.

meme based on a hasty and incomplete reading of the relevant texts, one that was initially propagated by Catholic scholars influenced by Mann's work, and which ultimately found its way into homosexual revisionist literature. The most important claim, which is first advanced by Mann and echoed in every version of the rejection thesis, is that Pope Leo IX resisted Damian's supposedly harsh recommendations and decided to respond with more leniency. However, the claim that Damian recommended harsher measures than those adopted by Leo is easily disproved by reference to Damian's clear statements in the final chapter of the *Liber*, in which he explicitly asks the pope to distinguish between different grades of sodomy in determining punishments, offering the possibility of penance and restoration to the clerical state for those who fall into the lesser degrees of the sin. This is, in fact, precisely what the pope does in his response to Damian, following his suggestions almost to the letter, although the pope's own scheme is slightly *more* severe than Damian's. As noted previously, Damian suggests that the pope determine the degree of the punishment based on the number of accomplices and the degree of its severity, while Leo adds to this a third criterion, which is the length of time during which the perpetrator was engaged in the behavior. This means that even solitary masturbation or femoral sodomy with few accomplices, if it has been a long-standing habit, would result in the permanent loss of ecclesiastical order, an outcome that Damian's proposed scheme did not imply.

Mann's confusion seems to have arisen from reading Leo's letter without sufficiently consulting the *Liber Gomorrhianus* for context, but it may also have resulted from an incomplete reading of the work itself, namely Damian's argument, advanced in chapters 14–16, that ancient canon law requires the dismissal from the priesthood of anyone who has ever committed an act of sodomy. However, this point seems to be made only for rhetorical purposes, to establish the gravity of the crime and the laxity implied by what seem to be spurious canons inserted into legal texts, and it is clearly contradicted by Damian's final suggestion that the pope show leniency for lesser grades of sodomy. This should be unsurprising, because Damian's recommendations for graded leniency in the *Book of Gomorrah* is reflective of his approach to other types of clerical corruption of the time, particularly simoniacal ordination. Although according to the letter of the law such illicit ordinations would normally require the degradation of a priest from his grade of order (a measure often demanded by indignant laity and clergy at the time), Damian regards such a measure to be impossible on a large scale, and recommends restoration of those guilty of lesser grades of the offense after a period of penance.[32]

Although Damian does imply that the letter of the traditional penal canons of the Church would not permit anyone guilty of any act of sodomy to return to the clerical state, he repeatedly implies that his own approach would not be as strict. For example, in chapter 3 he complains that permissive prelates hold that "he who is known to have fallen into this evil with eight, or even ten others who are equally filthy, nonetheless should be considered to remain in his order," qualifying the prohibition by the frequency of the sin, and in chapter 4, he condemns the notion that those who are "habitually corrupted" by sexual perversion should be admitted to the clerical state or permitted to remain there, rather than seeking to exclude all of those who have ever committed such acts.

---

[32] See for example, Damian's approach to simoniacal ordinations in Milan, in his letter 65 in *Reindel*, vol. 2, 246.

Moreover, as I indicate in a footnote to Leo's letter, the phrase cited by Mann to justify the notion that Leo rejected Damian's severity, *nos humanius agentes* ("we, acting more humanely") is not a barb directed against Damian at all, but rather an ironic use of the Council of Ancyra's own language to dispense from the severity of the same council's penal canons, which were cited by Damian to indicate the rigor of the ancient law. The Council of Ancyra, held in 314, had itself lessened the penalty of perpetual excommunication applied by previous councils, such as the Council of Elvira, to perpetrators of infanticide or abortion, using language very similar to that adopted by Leo in his letter to Damian. In Ancyra's canon 2, the council is quoted as decreeing: "Regarding women who fornicate, and kill their newborns, or who cause the conceived to be expelled [from the womb], the ancient definition removes them from the Church until the end of their lives. However, we define more humanely ..."[33] The structure of this expression is unmistakably replicated by Leo, who writes, "In accordance with the dictates of justice, all those who are polluted with the filthiness of any of the aforementioned four types are expelled from all of the grades of order of the immaculate Church, both in our own judgment and in that of the sacred canons. However, we, acting more humanely, wish and so order ..." Apparently, it was the same misreading of Leo's statement that led Bailey and Payer to conclude that Damian had even been "rebuked" by Leo, a claim that is particularly difficult to reconcile with the fact that Leo uses the most superlative expressions to praise Damian, even predicting his heavenly coronation.

---

[33] From the ancient translation of the council by Dionysius Exiguus (PL 67, 154C–D).

The additional claim made by Mann (and echoed by Toke, Bareille, Bailey, and Payer) that the pope somehow turned against Damian in response to a critical backlash to the work is based on a highly conjectural reading of Damian's Letter 33, written to Leo at an unknown date.[34] Although it is clear from the letter that Damian believed that the pope had been influenced by a whispering campaign against him, it contains no indication of the motive of the campaign, stating only that it is orchestrated by those who oppose his reforming zeal.[35] However, Damian was not only battling against the sin of sodomy, but even more so against clerical marriage and concubinage, as well as simoniacal ordinations, all of which undoubtedly provoked much enmity against him by Italy's often corrupt clergy. It is therefore pure conjecture to claim that the pope had turned against Damian because of the *Book of Gomorrah*, a conjecture that Mann advances as fact.[36]

Although letter 33 indicates that the relationship between Damian and Leo had been harmed by Damian's detractors, it is not at all clear that the falling out was permanent. Other letters written by Damian during Leo's pontificate indicate a strong working relationship in which Leo made Damian his

[34] Kurt Reindel believes it was written between sometime between 1050 and 1054 (*Riendel*, vol. 1, 332).

[35] See letter 33 in *Reindel*, vol. 1, 332–333.

[36] Franz Neukirch, *Das Leben des Petrus Damiani* (Göttingen, 1875), 55, also disputes this claim, which had been made centuries earlier by Caesar Baronius in the *Annales Ecclesiastici*, noting the pope's very strong support for Damian in his letter of response to the book. Some scholars have attached importance to Damian's citation of a verse of Scripture related to Sodom and Gomorrah in this letter (Gen. 18:20–21), but his reference is not to the vice, but to the example of God investigating complaints before acting upon them. This reference would be incongruous if Damian were defending the *Book of Gomorrah*, given that he is the accuser in that letter.

official representative for the purpose of resolving controversies, a role Damian would also play in other pontificates as well. If these letters were written after letter 33, then the relationship was restored fairly quickly, and this would seem to be confirmed by the fact that Leo's successors made Damian a cardinal bishop and entrusted him with the highest responsibilities. However, the order of the letters is impossible to determine with certitude.

The strange claim made by Boswell and repeated approvingly by Ranft that "Peter in fact had no luck in convincing anyone that gay sexuality deserved hostile attention," is belied not only by the effusively positive reception on the part of Leo in his letter to Damian and the penal decree decreed by the pope, but also by the fact that in the same year of the publication of the *Liber Gomorrhianus* (1049 according to Reindel), Leo presided over a French reform council that decreed that sodomy be punished with the most severe of ecclesiastical penalties. According to the text of the acts contained in the *Annales Ecclesiastici*, the council, held in Rheims in the latter half of 1049, directed that "sodomites" were to be treated like heretics and excommunicated from the Church.[37] Leo therefore decreed punishments for sodomy in both France and Italy following reception of Damian's work, hardly evidence that he didn't take Peter's concerns seriously.

Finally, the claim made by Boswell that Pope Alexander II stole the *Book of Gomorrah* from Damian can only be judged

---

[37] Caesar Baronius, *Annales Ecclesiastici*, vol. 17 (Paris, 1869), 30. The text describing the canons includes an excommunication against those guilty of heresy or of cooperating with heretics: "And because new heresies have arisen in Gaul, [the council] excommunicated them, adding those who accept an office or service from them, or who give any kind of defense to them," followed by: "It condemned Sodomites in the same way" *(Pari modo damnavit et Sodomitas)*. Translation mine.

to be utterly baseless, predicated on an even more conjectural reading of Damian's Letter 156. In this letter, which was written twenty years after the publication of the *Book of Gomorrah*, and which is one of the strangest in his corpus, Damian complains that Alexander took a book from him that was of great value and refused to give it back to him for some unstated reason, having locked it away. He does not name the book and does not even indicate clearly that the book was of his own authorship. Boswell has no way to know that the book was the *Liber Gomorrhianus*, a most unlikely conjecture given that the book had already been published twenty years earlier, and confiscating it would be of no use for purposes of censorship. Moreover, we have no reason to believe that Alexander would have objected to the contents of the book, particularly in light of the fact that he was a strong supporter of Damian's crusade to reform the sexual morals of clergy and laity.

Upon examination, the rejection thesis can only be seen as an accident of history, a tenuous meme based on hasty scholarship that is unsupported by—and even clearly contradicts—the historical evidence contained in the *Book of Gomorrah* and Damian's other letters, Leo IX's letter of endorsement, and other supporting documentation from the period.

Sources and Methods of the Translation

I have based my translation of the *Liber Gomorrhianus* on the critical edition of Damian's letters produced by the German historian Kurt Reindel and published by *Monumenta Germaniae Historica* in four volumes from 1983 to 1993. Reindel's edition is based principally on manuscripts dating from the eleventh and twelfth centuries and contains a thorough critical apparatus that includes variant readings and copious annotations.

Until the publication of Reindel's edition, the only version of Damian's letters available to the general public was the edition of Constantine Gaetani, a Benedictine monk who produced an *Opera Omnia* of Damian at the behest of Pope Clement VIII. It appeared in multiple volumes published in Rome from 1606–1615 and was republished many times, finally appearing (with numerous typographical errors) in J. P. Migne's *Patrologia Latina*. Although Gaetani's work was of great value in its day, Reindel's edition is vastly superior. While Gaetani does not indicate his manuscript sources, it seems that he (or his assistants) made significant modifications to Damian's original text, deleting some sentences and heavily modifying others in order to blunt the impact of his frank and descriptive language, and in some cases, to correct what the editors perceived as grammatical errors in Damian's Latin. In many cases these errors are not errors at all, but represent a sophisticated usage of Latin that escapes the editor's understanding; only in a handful of cases does he seem to offer a useful correction. The choice of Reindel over Gaetani was therefore an obvious one. I have not, however, rigorously followed the paragraph scheme of Reindel and have divided his longer paragraphs so as to maximize the readability of the text.

I have translated the chapter titles that appear in the earliest manuscripts that contain such titles (most of which are from the eleventh century), and have applied the earliest chapter numbering scheme that appears in the manuscripts, which differs somewhat from Gaetani's version and dates from the thirteenth century. In accordance with the medieval custom (which seems to date from the 11th century), I have placed Pope Leo IX's commendatory letter in response to the book at the beginning of the text.

For the purpose of translating Damian's Scripture citations I used the original Douay-Rheims translation of the Bible (published in stages in 1582, 1609, and 1610) as well as the modified version of the Douay-Rheims published in various editions by Bishop Challoner in the mid-eighteenth century. They are respectively designated by "DR" and "DRC" in the footnotes. When quoting the Scripture I normally used the latter source, placing "DR" after the footnote citation if I used the former instead. The original Douay-Rheims is a direct translation from an edition of Jerome's Vulgate that is quite close to the Clementine Vulgate, which sometimes made it preferable to the Challoner revision. However, Challoner's alterations more often rendered the verses more readable without departing from the Vulgate, and in those cases I selected it over the original Douay-Rheims. Any variations between the Clementine Vulgate and Damian's version are noted.[38]

Two other translations of the *Liber Gomorrhianus* into English precede my own. The first was produced by Pierre Payer, a professor of philosophy at Mount Saint Vincent University (now retired). Payer's edition is undoubtedly useful—particularly his introductory review of the history of Catholic legislation on sodomy—but is unfortunately based on the flawed edition of Gaetani and incorporates Gaetani's alterations and occasional mangling of Damian's Latin. Moreover, it approaches the work principally as a historical curiosity of interest to scholars investigating medieval attitudes towards homosexuality, rather than a work of theology that continues to be relevant to the modern Church.

The second translation available in English was produced by Damian scholar Owen Blum, a Franciscan who was devoted

---

[38] It should be noted that I modernized the spelling of quotations from the original Douay-Rheims, but otherwise left the text intact.

to the saint and reportedly aided Reindel in the creation of
the critical edition of Damian's works. This translation appears in Blum's four-volume complete edition of Damian's
works in English, which is a useful resource for scholars who
are unable to read Damian's difficult Latin.[39] Unlike Payer's
translation, Blum's is based on Reindel's critical edition and is
therefore not hobbled by defective source material. However,
Blum chose to translate the *Liber Gomorrhianus* in a very free
style that is not always faithful to the original Latin text[40] and
often fails to capture the beauty of the author's exalted style.
Moreover, Blum's edition has no specific introduction to the
work explaining its historical context and theological signif-
icance, which would seem crucial for a proper presentation
of the work in the context of the contemporary crisis in the
Catholic priesthood.

It was therefore my view that, despite the usefulness of the
two existing English translations of the *Liber Gomorrhianus*,
neither of them met the need of a scrupulously accurate version that conveys the majestic beauty of Damian's original
Latin. My translation seeks to remedy this deficiency, rendering the text in a more traditional way that adheres more
closely to the grammatical structure of Damian's writing, and
using an elevated style of English that offers a more authentic

[39] Peter Damian, *The Fathers of the Church Medieval Continuation: The Letters of Peter Damian: 31–60,* trans. Owen J. Blum (Washington: Catholic
University of America Press, 1990).

[40] The inconveniences arising from Blum's imprecise and sometimes
erroneous translations is noted by Toivo J. Holopainen, "Mistakes in
some passages in O.J. Blum's translation (1998) of De divina omnipoten-
tia," a supplement to his article "Peter Damian" in *The Stanford Encyclopedia of Philosophy,* Winter 2012 ed., at plato.stanford.edu. The problematical
nature of Blum's "interpretive" style in his translation of the *Liber Gomorrhianus* is also noted by historian Glenn Olsen, *Sodomites,* 205.

sense of the saint's own elegant manner of expression. I have also included footnotes to enable the reader to fully understand the text in its historic context, to clarify obscure points, and to explain expressions and citations unfamiliar to the contemporary mind.

Although I have provided footnotes to the translation which I hope will be useful to scholars, the principal purpose of the work is to make the *Book of Gomorrah* accessible to a wide audience, not to provide original research. However, in order to present the work accurately in its context, I have found it necessary to register my objections, which are supported by some of my own research, to the false claim that Pope Leo IX somehow rejected the work. In addition, it may be notable to scholars that I have also discovered the hitherto unknown origin of two important quotations that appear in the book, which I briefly explain in the following section.

Two of Damian's Previously Unknown Sources Discovered

As noted above, the *Book of Gomorrah* quotes extensively from ecclesiastical authorities by way of reference works that were sometimes unreliable. Quotations that might have originated with a council of the Church or an obscure ecclesiastical writer were sometimes attributed to a famous Church Father or even to the Bible in such compilations. Damian's use of these imperfect sources led him to incorrectly attribute several of his quotations, two of which have remained a mystery to scholars.

The first is the following passage, which in chapter 22 Damian attributes to St. Bede the Venerable, the last of the Fathers of the Latin Church:

He who thus gives alms while not discharging his guilt, does not redeem his soul, which he does not restrain from vices. This is demonstrated by the actions of that hermit who, having many virtues, had entered into the eremitic life with a certain associate of his. The thought was injected into him by the devil that whenever his sexual passions were excited he should discharge his semen by the rubbing of his genital member, just as he might expel mucus from the nostrils. For this reason he was turned over to demons as he died, while his companion watched. Then the same companion, who was ignorant of his guilt, and recalling his virtuous exercises, almost despaired, saying, "Who can be saved, if this man has perished?" Then an angel standing by said to him, "Do not be troubled; for this man, although he did many things, has nonetheless soiled everything by that vice which the apostle calls impurity."[41]

This quotation is found nowhere in the extant works of Bede, and until now researchers have been unable to discover its origins. As I show in the corresponding footnote of my translation, the statement is in fact a composite of two different statements, the first a somewhat mangled quotation from the sixth century pope St. Gregory the Great (540–604), and the second from a commentary on the quotation, which appears to originate in a tenth century work of St. Odo of Cluny.

The first sentence of the passage, "He who thus gives alms while not discharging his guilt, does not redeem the soul which he does not restrain from vices,"[42] is an altered form of a statement from Gregory's *Moralia in Job* (Moral homilies on the Book of Job), where it appears as follows: "For he who always wishes to sin, and always to give alms, gives money in

[41] *Reindel*, vol. 1, 319. Translation mine.

[42] "Qui ita elemosinam tribuit, ut culpam non dimittat, animam non redimit, quam a vitiis non compescit."

vain, because he does not redeem the soul which he does not restrain from vices."[43] The origin of Damian's paraphrased version of this quotation seems clear: it appears verbatim in the *Collationes* of St. Odo, abbot of Cluny,[44] where it is explicitly attributed to Gregory's *Moralia* and is followed by Odo's own commentary, which appears in the next chapter immediately following the quotation.[45] The commentary is identical to the story of the monk provided by Damian in his quotation of "Bede." This, then, is the origin of the entire quotation.[46]

Following the publication of Odo's *Collationes*, his paraphrasing of Gregory's *Moralia* along with his commentary were published in other manuscripts without the chapter division distinguishing them, and without the correct attribution. I have found one example of this in *De Corpore et Sanguine Christi*,[47] a work by the tenth-century Italian bishop Gezo of Tortona, a contemporary of Odo. Gezo presents the quotation of Gregory with Odo's commentary under a single chapter heading, and includes no attributions whatsoever. It is in this composite form that the quotation made its way into Damian's library, although it is unclear if Damian had Gezo's

---

[43] "Nam qui et semper peccare vult, et quasi semper eleemosynam largiri, frustra pretium tribuit, quia non redimit animam, quam a vitiis non compescit."Lib. 12, cap. 51 (PL 75, 1013B).

[44] Lib. 3, cap. 25 (PL 133, 570C).

[45] Lib. 3, cap. 26 (PL 133, 570C–D). The similarity of this commentary by Odo has already been noted by Olsen, *Sodomites*, 272, note 31, although Olsen does not resolve the origin of the quotation attributed to Bede, nor its conflation with Odo's commentary.

[46] This correlation with Gregory's *Moralia* was simultaneously discovered by Gianandrea de Antonellis, whose Italian translation of the *Liber Gomorrhianus* was also published this year by Edizioni Fiducia.

[47] Cap. 60 (PL 137, 403A).

work or another work reproducing the text in a similar way. How it was ultimately attributed to Bede is also a mystery.

Reindel's critical edition of the *Liber Gomorrhianus* and the translations of Blum and Payer have treated the first sentence of the text as a quotation of unknown origin, and the rest of the text as Damian's own commentary on the quotation. However, Gaetani presents the entire text as a quotation offered by Damian and attributed to Bede, without adding any citation of the works of Bede to substantiate it. Both of these approaches have an element of truth; the original quotation was distinct from the commentary, but Damian's source conflates them and he quotes them together as a single text.

The second quotation in question presents a similar problem. In chapter 24 of the *Book of Gomorrah,* Damian writes:

> How, I ask, are you able to despair of the abundant mercy of the Lord, who even rebuked Pharaoh, because he did not flee to the remedy of penance after sinning? Hearken to what he says: "I have crushed the arms of Pharaoh, king of Egypt, and he has not asked to be given health, and for strength to be returned to him for grasping the sword."

This appears to be simply Damian's own text followed by a Scripture quotation, which is a rough paraphrasing of Ezechiel 30:21.[48] However, the same paraphrasing appears word-for-word in a citation in Burchard of Worms' *Libri Decretorum,*[49] accompanied by a similar comment. Burchard in

---

[48] Damian's quotation reads: "I have crushed the arms of Pharaoh, king of Egypt, and he has not asked to be given health, and for strength to be returned to him for grasping the sword." The Clementine Vulgate reads: "Son of man, I have broken the arm of Pharaoh king of Egypt: and behold it is not bound up, to be healed, to be tied up with clothes, and swathed with linen, that it might recover strength, and hold the sword."

[49] Lib. 19, cap. 48 (PL 140, 994C).

turn attributes the quotation to St. John Chrysostom writing to Theodore of Mopsuestia. Researchers have been unable to locate this quotation in the writings of Chrysostom, but I have found that it occurs virtually verbatim in *De Reparatione Lapsi* (On the Reparation of the Lapsed), a work of the early fifth century ecclesiastical writer Bachiarius of Spain:

> How, I ask, can we despair of the mercy of the Lord, who even rebuked Pharaoh, [asking him] why he was not worthy by any means of doing penance, saying through the prophet of Pharaoh: "I have crushed the arms of Pharaoh, king of Egypt, and he has not asked to be given health, and for strength to be returned to him for grasping the sword."[50]

This text includes the same paraphrasing of Ezechiel 30:21, with a similar antecedent comment, making it almost certain to be the true origin of the quotation. Three chapters earlier in his own work, Burchard attributes another quotation from Chrysostom to Bachiarius's *De Reparatione Lapsi*, although in fact that quotation does not appear Bachiarius's work; perhaps Burchard or a later editor confused the two texts.

---

[50] Bachiarius, *De Reparatione Lapsi*, cap. 11 (PL 20, 1048A). Translation mine. The Latin text is precisely the same as it later appears in Book 19 of Burchard's *Libri Decretorum*: "Qualiter, rogo, de misericordia Domini possumus desperare, qui etiam Pharaonem arguit, quare nequaquam poenitere dignatus sit, dicens in propheta Pharaonis : Brachia regis Egypti contrivi ; et non est deprecatus ut daretur in eo sanitas, et redderetur ei virtus ad comprehendendum gladium."

THE LETTER OF POPE LEO TO PETER DAMIAN FOLLOWING THE BOOK OF GOMORRAH, CONFIRMING IT BY HIS APOSTOLIC AUTHORITY

Leo,[1] Bishop, Servant of the Servants of God, to the beloved son in Christ, Peter the hermit: the joy of eternal beatitude.

O most beloved son, this little book which you have written in a worthy style—but with even more worthy reasoning—against the four forms of polluted carnal intercourse, offers clear evidence to commend the effort of your soul to reach, through pious struggle, the splendid nuptial bed of shining chastity. You have subjugated the barbarity of the flesh, and you have thus raised the arm of the Spirit against the obscenity of lust. Indeed, accursed is the vice that distances one far from the Author of virtue, who, being pure, admits nothing unclean, and no one involved in filthy allurements can share in his fortune. The clerics, however, of whose most foul lives your prudence tearfully but equally rationally disputes, truly and altogether truly do not belong to his line of inheritance, from which they distance themselves by their pursuit of pleasures. If they were to live chastely, they would be recognized not only as the holy temple of the Lord, but even the sanctuary itself, in the snowy whiteness of which is immolated that illustrious Lamb of God by whom the filthy plague of the whole world is cleansed. Undoubtedly such clerics declare—not by the testimony of words, but of deeds—that they are

---

[1] That is, Pope St. Leo IX, Bishop of Rome from 1049 to 1054.

not what they are believed to be. For how may one be a cleric, or named as such, if according to his own judgment he does not fear to be soiled either by his own hands or those of another, fondling his own male parts or those of another, or fornicating with contemptible irrationality either between the thighs or in the rear?

Stirred up by holy rage, you wrote of such clerics according to your judgment; it is appropriate, as you desire, that we intervene with our apostolic authority so that we might dispel scrupulous uncertainty from the reader, and so that it may be known with certitude by all that everything that this little book contains has been pleasing to our judgment, being as opposed to diabolical fire as is water. Therefore, so that the license of foul lust may not spread unpunished, it is necessary that it be answered with a repression appropriate to apostolic severity, and yet that some moderation be applied to its harshness.

Behold: In accordance with the dictates of justice, all those who are polluted with the filthiness of any of the aforementioned four types are expelled from all of the grades of order[2] of the immaculate Church, both in our own judgment and in that of the sacred canons. We, however, acting more humanely,[3] wish and so order that those who have discharged semen

---

[2] This is a reference to the degrees or ranks of priestly ordination, including what are understood today as the major orders (bishop, priest, and deacon) and subdiaconate and minor orders (acolyte, exorcist, lector, and porter).

[3] Here Leo is alluding to an expression used by the Council of Ancyra (314) (whose texts are cited by Damian in his work) which substitutes a more lenient penance in place of perpetual excommunication (which was decreed at other councils, such as Elvira) in cases of infanticide and abortion. In the Latin translation of the council's canons by Dionysius Exiguus (PL 67, 154C–D) the council's canon 21 is quoted as stating: "Regarding women who fornicate, and kill their newborns, or who cause

either with their own hands or with others, or even have copulated between the thighs, and not for long periods of time nor with many people, if they curb this sensuality and atone for their shameful deeds with a worthy repentance, be admitted to those grades of order which they had occupied—but in which they did not remain—while in sin, being entrusted to divine mercy. For all those who have been polluted with either of two kinds of filthiness you were describing,[4] for long periods by themselves or with others, or with many others even for a short time, or—horrible to speak of and to hear—have fallen into corruption involving their rear end, the hope of recovering their order is lost.

If anyone dares to condemn or assail our decree of apostolic sanction, he should know that he is in danger of losing his own grade of order. For he who does not attack a vice, but rather coddles it, is justly judged guilty of the death together with those who die by that vice.[5] But, O most beloved son, I rejoice unspeakably that whatever you have taught with your ability as a preacher, you also teach through the example of your life, for it is better to instruct by deed, than by word. You

---

the conceived to be expelled [from the womb], the ancient definition removes them from the Church until the end of their lives. However, we define more humanely ..." (translation mine). Leo's allusion to Ancyra is ironic, as he is applying the same principle to Ancyra itself, adopting a legal principle less stringent than that suggested by the council's own canons. See Translator's Preface for more on this question.

[4] Although Damian normally designates four categories of sexual perversion, the "two types" referred to here appear to collapse Damian's first two categories (solitary masturbation and mutual masturbation) into a single first category, while making "femoral intercourse" into a second category. Leo then adds the third category of anal sodomy, to make a total of three.

[5] This is a reference to the guilt of sin as a form of spiritual death (see Eph. 2:5; Col. 2:13).

will therefore obtain the palm of victory from God the Father, and you will rejoice in the celestial mansion with the Son of God and of the Virgin, heaped up with as many rewards as were taken by you from the snares of the devil,[6] with which you will have been associated and in a sense, crowned.

[6] That is, souls saved from damnation.

I

THE BEGINNING OF THE BOOK OF GOMORRAH, BY THE HUMBLE MONK PETER DAMIAN

Peter, the least servant of monks, to the most blessed Pope Leo, the submission of due honor.

As the Apostolic See is known from the very mouth of the Truth[7] to be the mother of all of the churches,[8] it is proper to have recourse to it as a teacher and in a certain sense as the fount of heavenly wisdom, if some matter of doubt arises anywhere that seems related to the care of souls. Thus, from that one head of ecclesiastical discipline the light might show forth by which, the darkness of ambiguity having been expelled, the whole body of the Church will shine with the clear splendor of the truth. Moreover, a certain most abominable and exceedingly disgraceful vice has grown in our region, and unless it is quickly met with the hand of strict chastisement, it is certain that the sword of divine fury is looming to attack,[9]

---

[7] That is, Christ, who is "the way, the truth, and the life" (John 14:6).

[8] See Matthew 16:18, in which Christ designates the apostle Peter, who died as the head of the Roman Church, as the "rock" on which the Church is built, and gives him the keys to the kingdom of heaven.

[9] While Gaetani's version here has *grassaturus impendet* ("prepares to attack/run riot"), Reindel's critical edition, based on the earliest manuscripts, has *crassaturus impendet* ("prepares to thicken"). Given that Damian seems repeatedly to use *crassari* with the same meaning as *grassari*, Gaetani's correction seems to be justified, and I have used it here.

to the destruction of many. Alas, it is shameful to speak of it! It is shameful to relate such a disgusting scandal to sacred ears! But if the doctor fears the virus of the plague, who will apply the cauterization? If he is nauseated by those whom he is to cure, who will lead sick souls back to the state of health?

The cancer of sodomitic impurity is thus creeping through the clerical order, and indeed is raging like a cruel beast within the sheepfold of Christ with the audacity of such liberty, that for many it would have been much more salutary to be oppressed by the yoke of worldly duties than to be surrendered so freely to the iron rule of diabolical tyranny under the pretense of religion. It would have been better to perish alone in secular dress than, having changed one's clothes but not one's heart, to also drag others to destruction, as the Truth testifies, saying, "He that shall scandalize one of these little ones that believe in me, it is expedient for him that a millstone be hanged about his neck, and that he be drowned in the depth of the sea."[10] And unless the force of the Apostolic See[11] opposes it as quickly as possible, there is no doubt that when it finally wishes for the unbridled evil to be restrained, it may not be able to halt the fury of its advance.

---

[10] Matt. 18:6 (DR).

[11] That is, the see of the apostle Peter, the papacy.

II

ON THE DIFFERENT TYPES OF SODOMITES

So that the whole matter might be presented to you in an orderly way, I distinguish four types[12] of this nefarious sin. Some pollute themselves,[13] others are soiled by fondling each other's male parts, others fornicate between the thighs or in the rear, and these ascend by grades, such that each one is worse than the previous. Accordingly, the penance that is imposed on those who fall into sin with others is greater than those who dirty themselves alone by the discharged contagion of semen, and those who contaminate others in the rear are more strictly judged than those who copulate between the thighs. The skilled machination of the devil thus contrives these grades of corruption, so that the more it ascends them, the more deeply the unhappy soul may be plunged into the depths of hell.

[12] Damian makes use of this fourfold gradation of sexual perversion for most of the work, although he occasionally also addresses the sin of bestiality, which he regards as slightly less evil than anal sodomy (see chapter 7), as well as the sin of contraception, which he also sees as a form of sodomy (see chapter 4).

[13] That is, they engage in masturbation.

III

THAT EXCESSIVE MERCY LEADS SUPERIORS TO NOT PROHIBIT THE FALLEN FROM HOLY ORDERS

It is true that those who are guilty of this perdition often recover by the gift of divine mercy, arrive at satisfaction, and undertake the burden of penance—however heavy it might be—with devotion. However, they recoil in horror from the loss of ecclesiastical order. For certain prelates of churches—who are perhaps more merciful regarding this vice than is expedient—decree absolutely that no one may be deposed as a result of those three grades of sin which were enumerated above; they only allow those to be removed who are known to have copulated in the rear. That is, if one ejaculates semen by his own genital pressure, if he pollutes another by rubbing with his own hands, if he even lies between the thighs in the manner of those of the opposite sex, but he merely hasn't entered in the rear, he must receive a penance commensurate to the offense, but must not be removed from his order. So it is that he who is known to have fallen into this evil with eight or even ten others who are equally filthy, nonetheless should be considered to remain in his order.[14]

Such impious piety, without a doubt, does not reduce the wound, but administers a stimulus for its enlargement.[15] It

---

[14] That is, his priestly grade of order.

[15] The Latin here literally reads "but provides kindling so that it might be enlarged."

does not supply the bitterness of the illicit audacity that is perpetrated but rather grants the liberty of perpetrating it. Obviously, the carnal man of any order fears more to be despised in the sight of men than to be condemned according to the determination of the supreme Judge, and for this reason he would prefer any penance, however severe and extended it might be, to being subject to the endangerment of his grade.[16] Moreover, while he does not fear losing his honorable state by his indiscreet discretion, he is also inclined to take up new vices[17] and to remain longer in those he has taken up with impunity, so that, so to speak, as long as he is not struck where it hurts more severely, he lies serenely in that pigsty of filthy obscenity in which he first fell.

[16] That is, to the danger of losing his grade of order.

[17] The word translated as "new vices" is *inexperta*, which literally means "untried / unexperienced things."

IV

THAT THOSE WHO ARE HABITUATED TO FILTHY ENJOYMENTS SHOULD NOT BE PROMOTED TO HOLY ORDERS, NOR SHOULD THEY SO REMAIN IF THEY HAVE ALREADY BEEN PROMOTED

It seems to us exceedingly absurd that those who are habitually corrupted by this festering contagion should dare to be promoted to a grade of order or to continue in the grade to which they were already promoted. It is proven to be both contrary to reason and adverse to the canonical sanctions of the Fathers. However, I do not assert this in order to offer a definitive sentence in the presence of your majesty, but rather that I might explain the choice of a particular opinion.

Certainly, this disgrace is not unworthily believed to be the worst of all offenses, since tradition holds that the omnipotent God has always regarded it as hateful, and when he had not yet placed a legal precept prohibiting it along with the other vices he was already condemning it with the censure of strict retribution—not to mention that he destroyed Sodom and Gomorrah,[18] which were two distinguished cities, and all the neighboring regions, with sulfur and fire sent from heaven. He struck Onan, the son of Jude, with an untimely death because of this nefarious offense, according to the Scripture, which says, "Onan … knowing that the children should not be his, when he went in to his brother's wife, he spilled his

[18] Cf. Gen. 19.

seed upon the ground, lest children should be born in his brother's name. And therefore the Lord slew him, because he did a detestable thing."[19] Moreover, in the law it is said, "He that lieth with a man as if he should company with woman, both have committed abomination, dying let them die, their blood be upon them."[20]

That those who have fallen into that crime must not be promoted to ecclesiastical order because the old law decrees that it is to be punished with death, is attested by the blessed pope Gregory,[21] who in his letters writes to the bishop Passivus, stating:

> Your Fraternity[22] well knows how long Aprutium has been destitute of pastoral care; we have long sought after the one who should be ordained there and could not at all find him. However, because Importunus[23] is exceedingly praised to me in his morals, his zeal of psalmody, and his love of prayer, and he is said to live the religious life, we desire that your Fraternity bring him to yourself and that you admonish his soul so that it might grow in zeal for the good, and if no sins are found in him, which by the rule of sacred law are penalized by death, then he is to be

[19] Gen. 38:9–10.

[20] Lev. 20:13 (DR).

[21] That is, St. Gregory the Great, pope from 590 to 604.

[22] A respectful form of address used often by Gregory in his correspondence with bishops.

[23] The name of Gregory's candidate for the episcopate, here given as *Importunus*, appears in other manuscripts as *Opportunus* (cf. PL 77, 1226, footnote c). The difference between the two names is rather ironic. *Opportunus* in Latin means "fit, meet, convenient, suitable, seasonable, opportune" according to Lewis and Short, while *importunus* means the opposite.

ordained,[24] so that he be made either a monk or a subdea-
con for you, and after some length of time, if it pleases
God, he should be promoted to pastoral care.[25]

Behold, here it is clearly implied that any man who engages
with another man in feminine copulation; that is, between
the thighs—indeed which sin, as we taught above, is by the
sentence of the ancient law penalized with death—even if he
abounds in upright morals, is fervent with the zeal of psalm-
ody, is outstanding in the love of prayer, and leads an entirely
religious life according to the testimony of proven reputation,
can indeed fully receive the pardon of his guilt, but to ecclesiastical order he cannot at all be permitted to aspire. For regarding that venerable man Importunus, who at first is exalted
with such fervor of praise, is redeemed by so many ornaments
of a religious and upright life, and is decorated with so much
virtue of preaching, it is nevertheless added: "If they find no
sins in him, which by the rule of sacred law are penalized by
death, then he is to be ordained."

It is certainly obvious that no subsequent religious life can
restore a man for the reception of an ecclesiastical grade of
order if he has been debased by a crime worthy of death. Nor
does it enable him who is not doubted to have fallen into
the pit of mortal sin, to rise to attain the height of honor.
Therefore it is clearer than light that it is altogether against the
norm of sacred law, altogether against the standard of divine
authority, to promote anyone to ecclesiastical order who has
been convicted of having lain between masculine thighs in
fornication, which is undoubtedly a mortal sin.

[24] The phrase "then he is to be ordained" does not appear in Gregory's
letter as published in the *Patrologia Latina*.

[25] *Libri Epistolorum Sancti Gregorii Papae,* lib. 12, ep. 12 (PL 77,
1226B–1227A).

V

WHETHER IT IS LEGITIMATE FOR SUCH PEOPLE TO ACT AS PRIESTS IF THE CHURCH HAS NEED OF IT

However, it might be said that the need is pressing, that no one is available to carry out sacred duties in the Church, and appropriately the sentence which previously was pronounced by the dictate of stern justice is softened out of present necessity. To this I briefly respond: was there not also a necessity when the Pontifical See was lacking a pastor?[26] Will judgment be suspended because of the usefulness of one man, while the same judgment is firmly maintained to the abandonment of an entire people, and will that which is not relaxed for the advancement of an innumerable multitude be violated for the convenience of a single person?

But now let the outstanding preacher step forward, and let what he believes about this vice be more clearly known. For he states in the Letter to the Ephesians: "For understanding know you this, that no fornicator, or unclean, or covetous person (which is the service of idols) hath inheritance in the kingdom of Christ and of God."[27] If, therefore, those who are unclean do not have any sort of inheritance in heaven, by what presumption, by what reckless contempt might they, even

---

[26] This seems to be a reference to recent papal interregnum between the death of Pope Damasus II in August of 1048, and the accession of Pope Leo IX in February of 1049.

[27] Eph. 5:5 (DR).

more, obtain authority in the Church, which is nothing less than the kingdom of God? Will not he who has disregarded the divine law by falling into wickedness also be unafraid of contemptuously ascending to an office of ecclesiastical dignity? He will spare himself nothing, because he is unafraid of disregarding God in every way.

But surely this law was especially created for those who violate it, according to Paul, who, writing to Timothy, says:

> The Law is not made to the just man, but to the unjust[28] ... to the impious and sinners, to the wicked and contaminate, to killers of fathers and killers of mothers, to murderers, to fornicators, to liers with mankind, to manstealers, to liars, to perjured persons, and what other thing soever is contrary to sound doctrine.[29]

Therefore, given that the law, as has been demonstrated, should be imposed on those who lie with males so that they will not dare to violate the sacred orders, by whom, I ask, will this law be upheld, if it is despised principally by those for whom it was created? And if perchance a person is said to be useful, it is right that the more skillfully he excels in intellectual endeavors, the more he should cautiously uphold the rule of authentic law. For whoever has better understanding is guilty of worse sin, because he who in his wisdom was able to avoid sin if he had so wished will inevitably merit punishment. For as James says, "To one ... knowing ... good, and not doing it: to him it is sin."[30] And the Truth says, "To whom more is

---

[28] The Clementine edition of Jerome's Vulgate has "and disobedient" *(et non subditis)* where I have placed the ellipsis.

[29] 1 Tim. 1:9–10 (DR).

[30] Jas. 4:17 (DR). Here the Clementine Vulgate has "therefore" *(igitur)* and "to do" *(facere)* in the spaces I have marked with ellipses.

entrusted, more from him should be required."[31] For if the order of ecclesiastical discipline is confused by educated men, it will be a wonder if it is upheld by the ignorant. For if one who is knowledgeable is inordinately led to holy orders, he is seen in a sense to pave the way of error, which he has undertaken to walk with the swollen foot of arrogance, for those who follow and, so to speak, are simpler. And he is not only to be judged for having sinned but also because by the example of his own presumption he has invited others to imitate his sin.

---

[31] This is a reference to part of Luke 12:48, which reads: "And everyone to whom much was given, much shall be required of him." The exact wording in Latin differs significantly from that of the Clementine Vulgate, and seems therefore to be simply a paraphrase from memory.

VI

THAT THOSE WHO DESIRE ORDINATION AFTER HAVING BEEN INVOLVED IN THIS VICE ARE OF A REPROBATE SENSE

For who would pass by with a deaf ear, indeed, who would not shudder to the bone at the fact that the same Paul, like a trumpet, cries out vehemently with regard to such men, stating, "God gave them up to the desires of their heart, unto uncleanness, to dishonor their own bodies among themselves"?[32] And a little later [he writes]:

> For this cause, God delivered them up to shameful affections. For their women have changed the natural use into that use which is against nature. And, in like manner, the men also, leaving the natural use of the women, have burned in their lusts, one towards another: men with men, working that which is filthy and receiving in themselves the recompense which was due to their error. And as they liked not to have God in their knowledge, God delivered them up to a reprobate sense, to do those things which are not convenient.[33]

For how is it that after such a grave lapse they seek so earnestly after the sublimity of ecclesiastical order? What should one suppose, what should one believe, if not that God has turned them over to a reprobate sense? Nor does he allow them to see, while under the influence of their sins, the things

[32] Rom. 1:24.
[33] Rom. 1:26–28.

that are necessary for them. For because the sun has set for them (He, that is, who ascends upon the west)[34] they have lost their inner eyes,[35] and they do not even manage to consider how serious the evils are that they have perpetrated by their impurity, nor still how much worse it is that they desire inordinately to possess a grade of order against the will of God. In accordance with divine justice, those who soil themselves with this ruinous filth, having been struck with a fitting chastisement, always incur the darkness of blindness. Thus we read of those ancient originators of this foulness when they had "pressed very violently upon the just Lot, and were even at the point of breaking open the doors."[36] "And behold," says Scripture, "the men put out their hand, and drew in Lot unto them, and shut the door. And them, that were without, they struck with blindness from the least to the greatest, so that they could not find the door."[37]

It is certain, however, that the persons of the Father and of the Son are not inappropriately represented by those two angels who, we read, have come to the blessed Lot. This is made evident by what Lot himself says to them: "I beseech thee, my Lord, because thy servant hath found grace before thee, and thou hast magnified thy mercy, which thou hast

---

[34] Cf. Ps. 67:5 (Vulgate/Douay numbering): "Sing ye to God, sing a psalm to his name, make a way for him who ascendeth upon the west: the Lord is his name." The *Glossa Ordinaria*, the standard commentary on Scripture during the Middle Ages, cites Cassiodorus as associating this image with Christ, the "Sun of Justice" rising from the dead (an opinion shared by Pope St. Gregory the Great), hence Damian's metaphor of God as a "sun" that gives light to the soul. See *Bibliorum Sacrorum cum Glossa Ordinaria*, vol. 3 (Venice: 1603), 906.

[35] That is, their spiritual vision or understanding.

[36] The words "the just" *(iusto)* are not in the Clementine Vulgate.

[37] Gen. 19:9–11.

shewn to me in saving my life."[38] For when one addresses two singularly as if they were one, it is certain that he is venerating one substance in two persons. The sodomites, therefore, seek to violently burst in upon the angels, when impure men seek to approach God through holy orders. However, they are certainly struck by blindness because they fall into interior darkness by the just judgment of God, and thus they cannot even find the door; being separated from God by sin, they do not know the way back to it. For it is surely obvious that those who seek to approach God by the path not of humility, but of arrogance and vanity, do not discern where the way of entrance lies open, or that the door is Christ, as he himself said, "I am the door."[39] Those who lose Christ under the influence of sin fail to find the door through which they might enter the habitation of the heavenly citizens.

Therefore, they have been turned over to a reprobate sense, because as long as they do not measure the weight of their guilt in their own mind with careful consideration, they regard that most heavy load of lead as the lightness of empty punishment. The statement, "He struck those who were outside with blindness," the apostle manifestly declares when he says, "God delivered them up to a reprobate sense," and what is added, "so they would not be able to find the door," he also clearly explains when he says, "to do those things which are not convenient,"[40] as if he were to say, "so that they would try to enter where they should not."

For he who is unworthy of holy orders is attempting to force his way into the service of the holy altar—what is he doing if not striving to enter through the immovable obstacle of

[38] Gen. 19:18–19.
[39] John 10: 7, 9.
[40] Rom. 1:28.

a wall, having abandoned the threshold of the door? Because free entrance is not accessible by foot, such people, while they assure themselves that they may attain to the sanctuary, are frustrated in their presumption and are forced to remain in the exterior vestibule. They may strike their foreheads against the stones of Sacred Scripture, but they by no means are permitted to enter by the entranceway of divine authority, and when they try to enter where they are not permitted, they do nothing more than vainly grope the reinforced wall. To them the statement of the prophet is appropriately applied: "They shall … grope at noonday as in the night."[41] And those who are unable to cross the threshold of the proper entrance wander madly, whirling in a circle, of whom it is said by the psalmist: "O my God, make them like a wheel,"[42] and likewise: "The impious walk round about."[43] Regarding the same, Paul also, when he is speaking of the matters recounted above, a little later adds, "They who do such things are worthy of death: and not only they that do them, but they also that consent to them that do them."[44]

It is clear that if the thunder of apostolic invective does not awaken one to something so terrible, he should certainly be judged not as sleeping, but as dead. And given that the apostle so zealously augments a sentence of strict chastisement, not for Jews no matter how faithful, but for Gentiles and those who do not know God, what, I ask, would he have said, if he were to have seen this lethal wound festering in the very body of the holy Church? In particular, what grief, what fire

[41] Job 5:14.

[42] Ps. 82:14.

[43] Ps. 11:9. Perhaps a more precise translation would be: "the impious walk in a circle" *(in circuitu impii ambulant)*.

[44] Rom. 1:32.

of compassion would have inflamed that pious heart, if he were to have learned of this destructive plague festering even in sacred orders?

May idle prelates of clerics and priests hear! May they hear, and although they might be secure from personal guilt, may they fear themselves to be participants in the guilt of others! Undoubtedly, those who turn a blind eye to the sins of their subjects that they are obligated to correct, also grant to their subjects a license to sin through their ill-considered silence. May they hear, I say, and wisely understand, that all are uniformly worthy of death, indeed, "not only they that do them, but they also who consent to them that do them."[45]

---

[45] Damian is not, as some hostile commentators have claimed, recommending the death penalty for sodomy. He is quoting part of Romans 1:29–32, in which the St. Paul lists a large number of sins, including pride, disobedience to parents, dissoluteness, contumely, avarice, sodomy, and others, and concludes that "they who do such things, are worthy of death: and not only they that do them, but they also that consent to them that do them." The reference is to the gravity of the sin, not a recommendation for capital punishment by the state.

VII

ON RECTORS OF THE CHURCH
WHO ARE SOILED WITH THEIR
SPIRITUAL CHILDREN

O unheard of crime! O offense to be mourned with a whole fountain of tears! If they who consent to those who do these things are to be struck with death, what can be conceived of as a worthy punishment for those who commit these evils, which are punishable by eternal damnation,[46] with their spiritual children? What fruit can be found in the flocks, when the pastor is so profoundly submerged in the belly of the devil? Who might now remain under his rule who is not ignorant of his so hostile estrangement from God? Who makes a male prostitute out of penitent, a woman out of a man? Who subjugates as a slave him whom he spiritually generated as a son by God, through the iron rule of diabolical tyranny by the impurity of his flesh?[47]

If a man violates a woman whom he lifted from the sacred fountain,[48] is he not, without any obstacle of delay, judged to be deprived of communion and ordered by the censure of the sacred canons to suffer public penance? For it is written that

---

[46] The critical edition of Reindel lacks the word "punishable" (that is, *punienda*, or "to be punished"), which appears in Gaetani's edition. Reindel makes no note of the discrepancy, so it is unclear if he accidentally omitted the word or if Gaetani inserted it to make sense out of a phrase that would otherwise seem nonsensical.

[47] The word "who" *(quis)* in these last two sentences is intended to mean "What kind of person …?"

[48] That is, whom he baptized.

spiritual parenthood is greater than carnal parenthood. But he who receives one coming from the world into clerical orders has generated a spiritual child from God in almost the same way as he who might have baptized or received one raised from the baptismal font.[49] Indeed, the institution of canonical orders is a renunciation,[50] and is, in a certain sense, a second baptism.

It follows, therefore, both he who has ruined his carnal daughter, and he who has corrupted his spiritual daughter with sacrilegious intercourse, should suffer the same sentence, as well as he who pollutes, with abominable wantonness, a cleric whom he ordained—unless perhaps in this is the nature of the two crimes distinguished, that the first has sinned, although incestuously, yet naturally, because it was with a woman, while he who defiles a cleric has committed a sacrilege with his son, incurring the guilt of incest and dissolving the laws of nature.[51] And, as it seems to me, it is more tolerable to have fallen into the disgrace of lust with an animal than with a man. Indeed, how much more lightly is he judged who perishes alone, than he who drags another to the ruin of destruction! How miserable is the condition in which the ruin of one depends on another, and when one is destroyed, another follows necessarily to his death!

[49] These last two sentences appear to refer to the *Pontifical Book of the Church of Ravenna*, which states: "Greater is the spiritual father, than the carnal, because the first procreated his son in sin, and in sin was his son born to him, and the same son must die in sin. However, the spiritual father, after having received him from the baptismal water, the devil and all of his pomps having been taken away, generates a spiritual son from the sacred font." (PL 106, 520A). Translation mine.

[50] That is, a renunciation of worldly pursuits.

[51] Damian does not here intend to claim that incest as such is natural, only that heterosexual incest does not violate nature with regard to the complementarity of the sexes, a sin of which homosexual incest is additionally guilty.

VIII

OF THOSE WHO CONFESS THEIR OFFENSES TO THOSE WITH WHOM THEY HAVE FALLEN[52]

So that the deceits of diabolical machination may not lie hidden, but rather that I might expose to the light those things that the devil secretly constructs with his secretaries in the workshop of ancient evil, I will not suffer it to be concealed that certain individuals, satiated by the poison of this crime, when, as it were, they return to the heart,[53] confess the sin to one another so that the crime may not be exposed to the notice of others. Although as authors of the crime they cause the faces of men to blush, they themselves become judges, and each one rejoices to extend to the other an indiscreet pardon, which he seeks to apply to himself by vicarious exchange. So it is that they might be penitents of great sins, and yet their mouths are not pallid by reason of fasting, nor their bodies wasted by leanness; and while their stomach is in no way restrained from the immoderate reception of food, the soul is shamefully inflamed in the fire of habitual lust, so that he who has not yet wept for his crimes, commits even more lamentable acts.

---

[52] The act of hearing the confession of one with whom the confessor committed the sin in question continues to be prohibited in the Catholic Church's Code of Canon Law (c. 977), which invalidates such absolutions.

[53] That is, they repent. Cf. Isa. 46:8: "Return, ye transgressors, to the heart."

It is a precept of law[54] that when anyone is covered with leprosy he must be shown to the priests.[55] However, when one filthy man confesses to another the common evil that has been committed, the leper is not shown to the priests but rather to another leper. As a confession certainly should be a revelation, what, I ask, does he reveal, who narrates what is already known to his listener? Indeed, how is that confession to be made whereby nothing is revealed by the one who confesses except what is already known by the listener? Moreover, by what law, by what right can the one who is restrained by the social bond of an evil committed, bind and loose that of others? For in vain does he who is also bound by chains attempt to free another, and for him who wishes to lead a blind man on a journey it is necessary that he should see, that he may not cause the one who follows him to fall, as is said by the voice of the Truth, when he says, "If the blind leads the blind, both fall into the pit,"[56] and again, "Seest thou the mote in thy brother's eye: but the beam that is in thy own eye thou considerest not ... hypocrite, cast first the beam out of thy own eye: and then shalt thou see clearly to take out the mote from thy brother's eye."[57]

It is most openly declared by these evangelical testimonies, that he who is oppressed by the darkness of the same guilt, in vain seeks to restore another to the light of contrition, and if he does not fear to lead another by straying beyond his powers,[58] he does not evade the gaping pit of ruin, together with him who follows.

[54] That is, the Mosaic law of the Old Testament.

[55] Cf. Lev. 13:12–17.

[56] Matt. 15:14.

[57] Luke 6:42–42.

[58] This seems to be a reference to his power of granting absolution.

IX

JUST AS IS THE CASE WITH THOSE WHO VIOLATE NUNS, A PROSTITUTOR OF MONKS MUST BE DEPOSED IN ACCORDANCE WITH THE LAW

I now address you face to face, whoever you are, O sodomite. Do you refuse to confess your sins to spiritual men, because you also fear to lose your ecclesiastical rank? But how much more salutary would it be to endure temporal shame in the sight of men, than to suffer eternal punishment before the tribunal of the heavenly Judge?

Perhaps you might reply to me that if a man lies with a man only between the thighs he is certainly in need of penance, but in accordance with merciful kindness, he should not be permanently prohibited from his grade of order. I ask you, if a monk makes an attempt upon a nun, is he to remain in holy orders according to your judgment? But there is no doubt that you would judge that such a man be should be deposed! It therefore follows that what you reasonably assert regarding a nun you should inevitably admit of the monk, and what you would assert regarding monks it is necessary for you to apply to clerics, but, as was stated previously, with this difference: that the latter is to be considered worse, insofar as by the identity of the sexes it is judged to be contrary to nature.

Moreover, it is right to always consider the will of the offender when judging excesses, and he who pollutes masculine thighs, if nature were to permit, would carry out completely with men whatever is done with women in the insanity of unrestrained lust. He has done what he could, up to the point where nature has denied him, and he has there unwillingly fixed the boundary of his offense where the necessity of nature has placed the impassable limit of ability. Therefore, because the same law is applicable to monks of either sex, it is necessary to conclude that just as the violator of a nun is deposed by law, so also he who prostitutes a monk should be removed in all ways from his office.

X

THAT BOTH HE WHO FALLS WITH HIS CARNAL OR SPIRITUAL DAUGHTER, AND HE WHO IS SOILED WITH HIS PENITENTIAL SON, SHOULD BE ACCOUNTABLE FOR THE SAME OFFENSE

So to respond again to the disputations of the "sacred" (that is, detestable)[59] confessors: if any canonical priest falls with a woman to whom he has declared the verdict of penance[60] even once, no one denies that he should be removed from his grade of order by the censure of the synodal council.[61] If, however, he falls with a priest or a cleric of almost equal rank for whom he is either a judge in giving penance or has been judged in receiving it, will he not lose the honor of his order[62] in accordance with the dictates of justice? For it is customary to call him a "penitential son," just as we say "baptismal son." Thus it is read of blessed Mark the evangelist that "he is the

---

[59] This is a play on two possible meanings of the Latin word *sacer, sacris,* which can refer to the sacred, or to something accursed and therefore detestable. I have added quotation marks around the word "sacred" to indicate that it is to be read in an ironic sense.

[60] That is, to whom he has given a penance in sacramental confession.

[61] That is, removed from his grade of order in accordance with the laws established by the synods of the Catholic Church, a matter upon which Damian expounds at length in the following three chapters.

[62] That is, his grade of ecclesiastical order (e.g. bishop, priest).

son of Peter in baptism,"[63] and it is the eminent preacher who says, "For Christ sent me not to baptize, but to evangelize,"[64] and also says, "For what is my glory before the Lord? Is it not you?"[65] "For in Christ Jesus, by the gospel, I have begotten you."[66] And to the Galatians he says, "My little children, of whom I am in labor again, until Christ be formed in you."[67] If then he bore, if he gave birth—he who was not sent to baptize, but to evangelize and so to urge repentance—it is rightly said that he who receives penance is a son, and that he who imposes it is a father.

Now if the above-mentioned facts are carefully considered, it will be clearer than light that he who fornicates with either a carnal or a baptismal daughter is guilty of the same crime, and he also who acts indecently with a penitential son. And just as for him who has sinned with a female whom he generated carnally, or whom he birthed in baptism, or upon whom he imposed the judgment of penance, so also for him who sins with a penitential son through lust, it is just that he be removed in every way from the order of which he is a minister.

---

[63] This appears to be a quotation of a Monarchian Prologue to the Gospel of Mark, a text that dates from about A.D. 350 and appeared in many Latin Bibles of Damian's time.

[64] 1 Cor. 1:17 (DR).

[65] This seems to be a paraphrase from memory of 1 Thess. 2:19: "For what is our hope or joy or crown of glory? Are not you, in the presence of our Lord Jesus Christ at his coming?"

[66] 1 Cor. 4:15.

[67] Gal. 4:19.

XI

REGARDING APOCRYPHAL LAWS,
IN WHICH WHOEVER TRUSTS IS
ALTOGETHER DECEIVED

But because certain lullabies are found mixed with the sacred canons,[68] in which corrupt men place their confidence with vain presumption, we examine some here so that we may clearly demonstrate that not only they, but all other writings similar to them, wherever they might be found, are altogether apocryphal. For it is said, among other things: "A priest who has not taken the vow of a monk, who sins with a girl or a harlot, must do penance for two years, and for three Lents, on Monday, Wednesday, Friday, and Saturday, always with dry food; if it is with a female servant of God[69] or with a man a fast is added of five years, if it is habitual."[70] Similarly deacons, if they are not monks, as well as monks that are not in holy orders, [must do penance for] two years. A little later the

[68] That is, the canon law of the Catholic Church. The laws cited by Damian in the following chapters resemble closely those contained in the *Libri Decretorum* of Burchard of Worms, lib. 17, cap. 39–41 (PL 140 926C–927D), a widely-used medieval compilation of canon law and penances, although Damian appears to be using multiple sources which may only replicate some of the same texts. Damian's complaint about the unreliability of penitentiary books is an echo of other similar complaints made in the proceeding centuries (see Translator's Preface).

[69] That is, a nun. The same term is used for nuns in chapter 12.

[70] The Latin for "if it is habitual" is *si in consuetudine est*, which seems to have been used generally in canon law regarding the habitual or frequent commission of a sin.

following is inserted: "If a cleric who has not taken monastic vows commits an act of fornication, he must do penance for half a year; if he has done so frequently he must do a whole year of penance; if he is a canon,[71] likewise; if frequently, two years."

Likewise, if one sins in the manner of the sodomites, some dictate ten years of penance. He who does so habitually must be punished more. If he holds a grade of order, he must be degraded and do penance as a layman. A man who fornicates between the thighs must do one year of penance. If he repeats the offense, he must do penance for two years. If he fornicates in the rear, he must do three years of penance. If he is a child, he must do two years of penance. If he fornicates with a sheep or a mule, he must do ten years of penance. Likewise, a bishop who sins with quadrupeds must do ten years of penance and lose his grade of order; a priest, five years; a deacon, three; a cleric, two; and many other erroneous and sacrilegious machinations of the devil are found inserted into the sacred canons, which to us would be more pleasing to obliterate than to read—better to spit, than to write such vain foolishness on paper.

Behold, sodomites trust in these inanities; they give faith to them as to a portent from dreams and delude themselves with the assurance of a vain hope. But let us see if these agree with canonical authority, so that, whether they should be affirmed or rejected, they should be made known not so much by the testimony of words as by the testimony of facts.

---

[71] That is, a priest attached to the cathedral of a diocese or some other church served by priests living in community.

XII

THE JUSTIFIABLE REJECTION
OF THE ABOVE LAWS

Therefore, to return to the beginning of this deceptive law code, it is said that a priest who has not taken monastic vows, and who sins with a girl or with a harlot, must do two years of penance. And who is so stupid, who is so insane, to believe that a penance of two years for a priest caught in fornication is appropriate? For whether one has only a minimal acquaintance with canonical authority or the greatest knowledge, he would freely acknowledge that if a priest falls into fornication, a penance of at least ten years should be decreed,[72] not to mention stricter punishments. However, this penance of two years for fornication is not only not considered to be applicable to priests, but not even to the laity who, fleeing from this ruin to satisfaction,[73] are given a sentence of three years. Then the following is added: "If one sins with a female servant of God, or with a male (with the understanding that a priest is meant), a fast is added; that is, of five years, if it is habitual." Likewise deacons, if they are not monks, must do penance for two years, as also must monks who do not hold a grade of order.

---

[72] Burchard's *Libri Decretorum*, lib. 17, cap. 56 (PL 140, 931D) seems to reflect this principle, citing the Roman Penitential as decreeing a minimum of ten years penance for priests guilty of such sins.

[73] That is, the satisfaction of the requirements of penance.

I eagerly gaze upon one thing in the section of this non-sensical decree upon which I am expounding, gladly turning my attention to it, because it is clearly stated, "If … with a female servant of God, or with a male." Behold, O good man sodomite, in your own texts, which you so especially love, which you eagerly embrace, which you put forth as a shield of defense for yourself, you openly acknowledge that there is no difference if one sins with a female servant of God or with a male. However, for an equal sin there is the determination of an equal sentence. Now there is no basis for your disagreement with me, no way for you to rightly dissent from my arguments. Who is so out of his mind, who so profoundly incurs the darkness of blindness, that he would impose a penance of five years on a priest for sinning with a female servant of God (that is, a nun), or a penance of two years on a deacon or a monk? Is this not an insidious trap for the lost? Is this not a snare for straying souls? But who would be able to overrule what is stated—that a cleric who fornicates with a girl, if he hasn't taken monastic vows, must do half a year of penance? Who is so knowledgeable in Sacred Scripture, who stands out with such an abundance of expertise in dialectical subtlety, that he might presume to condemn such a law by the law itself, a blameworthy precedent whose authority is laudably detested? Whereas three years are given to the layman, for the cleric a half year of penance is prescribed? Blessed are the clerics who fornicate, if they are to be judged by the standards of sodomites; indeed, the same measure which they mete out to others, they wish to grant to themselves![74] This author of error, who extends the dogma of his perversity to the clerical

---

[74] This is an ironic reference to the Beatitudes (Matt. 5:1–12; Luke 6:20–23), and another aphorism from the Sermon on the Mount (Matt. 7:2; Luke 6:38).

order while he strives to ruin monks, is quite desirous of gaining souls for the devil, and because the death of monks alone cannot satisfy the gluttonous stomach of his malice, he desires to satisfy himself with the homicide of another class of souls.

Let us then see what follows: If one sins like the sodomites, certain authorities dictate ten years of penance. He who does so habitually must be punished more. If he holds a grade of order, he is to be degraded and do penance as a layman. If a man fornicates between the thighs, he must do penance for one year. If he does so again, he must do penance for two years. If, however, he fornicates in the rear, he must do three years of penance. And given that sinning like a sodomite, as you yourselves adduce, must be nothing other than to fornicate in the rear, why is it that your canons in just one sentence are so various and multifarious that they burden those who sin as sodomites with ten years of penance, but then for those who fornicate in the rear—which is the same thing—they confine the laments of penance within the space of three years? Are these things not rightly compared to monsters, not produced by nature, but composed by human industry, certain ones of which begin with equine heads and end with the hooves of goats?[75]

So, to which canons, to which decrees of the Fathers do these laughable things correspond, which clash with each other with such dissonant faces, as if they had horns on their heads? If they overthrow themselves, on what authorities can they rely? "Every kingdom divided against itself shall be brought to desolation; and house upon house shall fall. And if Satan be divided against himself, how shall his doctrine

---

[75] That is the Chimera, a monster depicted in Greek and Roman mythology and used often in medieval literature as a metaphor for the fictitious and non-existent.

stand?"[76] For first they seem to apply a strict punishment, then to exhibit a cruel mercy, and like a chimerical monster here a menacing species of lion roars, and there a vile she-goat humbly blesses, and by this diversity of various appearances they provoke laughter rather than inspiring penitential lamentation.

Those that follow are similarly erroneous: He who fornicates with sheep or a mule must do ten years of penance, and likewise a bishop who sins with quadrupeds must do ten years of penance and lose his grade of order; a priest, five; a deacon, three; a cleric, two.[77] As the previous sentence absolutely states that whoever fornicates with a sheep or a mule will be sentenced to ten years of satisfaction, how is it consistent to add that to a priest five years, a deacon three years, and a cleric two years of penance should be applied for sexual relations with livestock? So anyone—that is, any person, even if he is a layman—is punished with suffering for a period of ten years, and then five years is imposed on a priest; that is, half of the penance is eliminated!

I ask, to what pages of sacred eloquence coincide these tireless frivolities, which so evidently conflict with themselves? Who does not consider, who does not clearly see, that these and similar ones that are fraudulently mixed with these sacred canons are diabolical inventions and have been created for deceiving the minds of the simple by clever machination? For like honey or any tastier food, the poison is fraudulently admitted, so that while the sweetness of the food provokes one to eat, the poison, which lies hidden, enters more easily

---

[76] Cf. Luke 11:17–18. The Clementine Vulgate has "kingdom" rather than "doctrine" here.

[77] The word "cleric" here seems to refer to those who are studying in preparation to receive major orders, such as subdeacons, acolytes, etc.

into the entrails. Thus, these deceitful and erroneous inventions are inserted into the sacred texts so as to escape the
suspicion of fraud, and they are smeared, as it were, with a
certain kind of honey, appearing flavored with the sweetness
of a false piety. Avoid these things, whoever you might be, lest
the song of the Sirens charm you with fatal sweetness, lest it
plunge the ship of your soul in the chasm of the Scylla.[78] The
ocean of the holy councils should not perchance terrify you
with its manifest austerity, and the shallow sandbanks of the
apocryphal canons should not attract you with the promised
gentleness of their turbulence. For often a ship that is fleeing
the violent waves suffers a shipwreck as it approaches the
sandy shore, and often when it cleaves to the high sea, it escapes unscathed without the loss of a burden.

[78] In Greek mythology the Sirens are creatures whose seductive song
lure sailors to their deaths on rocky shores, and the Scylla is a multi-
headed monster that consumes sailors from ships that pass too close to
her dwelling place on the coast, pulling them into the chasm she inhabits.

XIII

THAT SUCH MOCKERIES ARE RIGHTLY EXCLUDED FROM THE LIST OF CANONS, BECAUSE THEIR AUTHORSHIP IS UNCERTAIN

Who fabricated these canons? Who has presumed to plant such spiny, such prickly thorn bushes in the purple grove of the Church? It is exceedingly clear that all authentic canons are either formulated in venerable synodal councils or are promulgated by the holy fathers who are pontiffs of the Apostolic See, and it is not licit for just anyone to eliminate canons, but rather this privilege is enjoyed only by those who are chosen to preside in the see of the blessed Peter. However, these spurious shoots[79] of canons of which we speak are both known to be excluded from the sacred councils and proven to be altogether alien to the decrees of the Fathers.[80]

It therefore follows that those that appear not to have been issued by decrees of the Fathers nor by sacred councils are by no means to be accepted among the canons. For whatever is not numbered among the species, is, without a doubt, determined to be alien to the genus. If the name of the author is sought, it cannot be identified with certainty, because it is not uniformly indicated in various books. For in

---

[79] This is a reference to the above metaphor of the "thorn bushes."

[80] That is, the Holy Fathers, the popes.

one it is attributed to Theodore,[81] in another, to the Roman
Penitential,[82] in another, to the Canons of the Apostles.[83] They
are titled one way here, another way there, and when they do
not have the merit of a single author, they undoubtedly lose
all authority. For those which waver between so many uncertain authorities confirm nothing with certain authority, and
it is necessary that those things that produce the darkness of
uncertainty for readers may recede far from all doubt by the
light of the Sacred Scriptures.

Now, with these theatrical absurdities, in which the sodomites have trusted, eliminated from the list of the canons
and convicted by the clear reasoning of arguments, let us
set out those canons of whose trustworthiness and authority
we have no doubt. Indeed, they are found in the Council of
Ancyra:[84,85]

---

[81] This appears to be a reference to Theodore, Archbishop of Canterbury (d. 690), who published a famous manual of penitential canons.

[82] Several medieval manuals of penitential canons bore this title. See
Philip Schaff, *History of the Christian Church*, vol. 4 (New York: Charles
Scribner's Sons, 1913), 371–374.

[83] The Canons of the Apostles or Apostolic Canons are a collection of
ancient ecclesiastical laws which formed part of the Apostolic Constitutions, a broader work summarizing Christian teaching first published in
the third century.

[84] A council held by Catholic bishops in the town of Ancyra in Galatia
(today Ankara, Turkey) in 314, the year following the end of the last persecution of Christians by Roman emperors. Among other matters, it prescribed various penances for those who had repudiated their faith during
the persecution of the emperor Diocletian and who wished to return to
communion, as well as penances for sexual misbehavior and other sins.
The council, in its Latin translations and interpretations, became an important source for medieval penitentiary manuals.

[85] The quotation of the Council of Ancyra follows at the beginning of
the next chapter.

XIV

OF THOSE WHO FORNICATE IRRATIONALLY; THAT IS, WHO MIX WITH ANIMALS OR ARE POLLUTED WITH MALES[86]

Regarding these who have lived irrationally or continue to do so: Those who have committed such a crime before age twenty may be admitted to the communion of prayer after having done fifteen years of penance. Then, after five years in this communion, they may finally receive the sacraments of offering.[87] However, their lives during the period of penance should be investigated before they obtain mercy, for if they insatiably adhere to these offenses, they should spend more time doing penance. Those who have reached twenty

---

[86] This is the title given in medieval collections of canon law, such as the *Collectio Dionysio-Hadriana,* the *Collectio Canonum Quadripartia,* the *Collectio Dacheriana,* and Burchard's *Libri Decretorum,* to the text of canon 16 of the Council of Ancyra, which immediately follows. The title applies the Greek for "those who have lived irrationally" (which is reported in different versions of the Greek canons as ἀλογευσαμένων [*Hefele,* 215] or ἀλογῶς διαγόντων [translation of Isidorus Mercator, PL 130, 265A]) to those guilty of bestiality or homosexual acts. Damian's source for the title is probably Burchard's *Libri Decretorum,* lib. 17, cap. 30 (PL 140, 924D–925A). Other Western canons seem to have been influenced by the same interpretation. Thus, as *Percival,* 70, notes, an English canon from the time of King Edgar which was based on this same canon reads "If any one twenty years of age shall defile himself with a beast, or shall commit sodomy, let him fast fifteen years ...."

[87] The "sacraments of offering" are the Eucharist or Holy Communion, which the Catholic Church understands as a sacrificial offering to God.

years of age and are married and fall into this sin must do twenty-five years of penance and are then received in the communion of prayer. After remaining in this state for five years, they may finally receive the sacraments of offering. But those who thus sin who have wives and have passed fifty years of age should receive the grace of communion[88] at the end of their lives. [89]

Behold, in the same inscription of this venerable authority we clearly see that not only those who fornicate in the rear, but also those who in any way are polluted with men, are compared in every respect with those who lie with animals. If we consider the interspersed words,[90] we perceive that they have been placed there carefully and with very judicious discernment, as it is stated, "Those who mix with animals or are polluted with males." For if with this phrase, "those who are polluted with males," it had intended to indicate those who fornicate in the rear,[91] it would not have been at all necessary for it to add two words, when only with "mix" it could have expressed its intention.

It would have sufficed indeed for brevity of style if the whole sentence had been composed with one verb, saying, "those who mix with animals, or males." For those who adulterate themselves in one sense are those who violate animals, and in another sense are those who violate males in the rear.

[88] That is, they should be given viaticum, the sacrament of Holy Communion received at the hour of death.

[89] This paragraph is canon 16 of the Council of Ancyra, which is almost identical to one given by Burchard in the *Libri Decretorum*, lib. 17, cap. 30 (PL 140, 924D–925A), which in turn was based on the translation of Dionysius Exiguus, who first translated the canon into Latin in the early sixth century (see the *Codex Canonum Ecclesiasticorum*, PL 67, 154C–D).

[90] That is, in the title of the canon.

[91] That is, *only* those who fornicate in the rear.

But, as it says that some mix with animals, others not "mix" but "are polluted" with males, it is surely clear that at the end of the phrase it passes judgment not on corrupters of males, but on "polluters." However, it should be noted that this regulation was principally instituted with regard to the laity, which is easily deduced from the words that follow: "Those who have committed such a crime before the age of twenty may be admitted to the communion of prayer after having done fifteen years of penance, then, after five years in this communion, they may finally receive the sacraments of offering."

If, therefore, any layman guilty of this crime is admitted to the communion of prayer after doing twenty-five years of penance but is not yet permitted to receive the sacraments of offering, how is it considered appropriate for a priest not only to receive but also to offer and to consecrate the sacred mysteries? If he is barely permitted to enter the church to pray with others, how is it that he can approach the altar of the Lord to intercede for others? If he does not have the right to hear the holy solemnities of masses before completing such a long period of penance, how is he worthy to solemnly celebrate them? If the former, who sinned less inasmuch as he walks the broad road of the world,[92] is unworthy of receiving in his mouth the heavenly offering of the Eucharist, how will the latter be worthy to handle such a terrible mystery with polluted hands? Let us consult again the same Council of Ancyra and what it ordained for the same crime:[93]

---

[92] This is a reference to Matthew 7:13: "Enter ye in at the narrow gate: for wide is the gate, and broad is the way that leadeth to destruction, and many there are who go in thereat."

[93] The quotation from the Council of Ancyra follows at the beginning of the next chapter.

XV

OF THOSE WHO WERE ONCE POLLUTED EITHER WITH ANIMALS OR WITH MALES, OR WHO CONTINUE TO LANGUISH IN THIS VICE[94]

"Those who have lived irrationally and have polluted others with the leprosy of this grave offense are ordered by the holy synod to worship with those who are vexed by an impure spirit."[95] As it plainly does not say those who "corrupt" others with the leprosy of this grave offense, but rather "pollute," (which also agrees with the preceding title itself, which begins not with those who have been "corrupted" but those who have been "polluted"), it is certainly clear that if a man in any way has been polluted with another man through the ardor of lust, he is ordered to pray not among Catholic Christians, but among the demonically possessed. For if sodomites are unable on their own to understand what they are, they might in any case be taught by those with whom they are consigned to the common penitentiary of prayer. And it certainly is proper enough that those who trade their flesh to demons through such foul commerce against the law of nature, against the

---

[94] This is the title given in medieval collections of canon law to the seventeenth canon of the Council of Ancyra (see translation of Dionysius Exiguus, PL 67, 154D).

[95] This is the text of canon 17 as it appears in Latin collections of medieval canon law. The source, again, is probably Burchard of Worms (*Libri Decretorum*, lib. 17, cap. 31; PL 140, 925B), who based it on the translation of Dionysius Exiguus (PL 67, 154D).

order of human reason, should receive a common place of prayer with the demonically possessed. For as human nature itself deeply resists these evils, and the lack of sexual difference is abhorrent, it is clearer than light that they never would have dared to engage in such perversities unless evil spirits had fully possessed them as "vessels of wrath, fitted for destruction."[96] But when they begin to possess them, they pour in the infernal poison of their malignity throughout the invaded heart that they fill, so that they might now eagerly desire not those things that a natural movement of the body demands, but that which only diabolic haste supplies. For when a man thrusts himself upon another man to commit impure acts, it is not from a natural carnal drive, but only the stimulus of diabolical impulse.

Thus the holy Fathers, in their vigilance, sentenced sodomites to pray together with those who are demonically possessed, those whom they did not doubt of having been invaded by the same diabolic spirit. Therefore, how can a mediator stand between God and the people in the dignity of the priestly office, who, separated from the congregation of the whole people, is ordered to only pray among demoniacs? But now that we have undertaken to apply two testimonies from one sacred council, let us also introduce what the great Basil thinks about that vice which is currently being addressed,[97] so that "in the mouth of two or three witnesses every word may stand,"[98] for he says:[99]

[96] Rom. 9:22.

[97] That is, St. Basil, Bishop of Caesarea Mazaca (370–79), a Father and Doctor of the Church.

[98] Matt. 18:16.

[99] The quotation follows at the beginning of the next chapter.

XVI

OF CLERICS OR MONKS
WHO PERSECUTE MALES

A cleric or monk who persecutes adolescents or children, or who is caught in a kiss or other occasion of indecency, should be publicly beaten and lose his tonsure, and having been disgracefully shaved, his face is to be smeared with spittle, and he is to be bound in iron chains, worn down with six months of imprisonment, and three days every week to fast on barley bread until sundown. After this, spending his time separated in his room for another six months in the custody of a spiritual senior, he should be intent upon the work of his hands and on prayer, subject to vigils and prayers, and he should always walk under the guard of two spiritual brothers, never again soliciting sexual intercourse from youth by perverse speech or counsel.[100]

Here the sodomite should zealously consider whether he whom sacred authority judges to be dishonored with such ignominious, such reproachful indignity, is safely able to carry

---

[100] This quotation, which Damian's source (probably Burchard's *Libri Decretorum*, lib. 17, cap. 35; PL 140, 925D) attributes to St. Basil, is in reality a slightly truncated form of a penalty prescribed for monks by St. Fructuosus of Braga (d. 665) (*Regula Monachorum*, cap. 16; PL 87, 1107A–B). A section of it also appears in the decrees of Ecgbert, bishop of York (d. 766) (PL 89, 387D), who correctly attributes it to Fructuosus, but in the later *Collectio Canonum Quadripartia*, (a manual used and referenced widely during the latter part of the early middle ages in France, England, and Italy), it contains no attribution. By the tenth century, collections of canon law such as Burchard's were incorrectly attributing it to Basil.

out ecclesiastical duties. Nor should he flatter himself for not having corrupted anyone in the rear, or for not having copulated between the thighs, when it is clearly written that he who is caught only in a kiss or other shameful occasion will be rightly subjected to all of those humiliations of shameful discipline.

For if a kiss is struck with a punishment of such severe retribution, what does fornication between the thighs merit? For punishing what crime, for what monstrous offense would it not suffice to be publicly beaten, to lose the tonsure, to be disgracefully shaven, to be smeared with the filth of saliva, to be confined for a great length of time, and furthermore to be bound in iron chains? And finally it is prescribed that he is to be fed on barley bread, because he who has become like a horse and a mule[101] is not properly refreshed with the food of men, but is fed with the grain of mules.

Moreover, if we fail to consider the weight of this sin, it is nonetheless clearly declared in the very judgment of penance which is imposed. For whoever is forced by canonical censure to submit to public penance is surely judged to be unworthy of ecclesiastical duties by the clear sentence of the Fathers. Thus the blessed Pope Siricius[102] among other things wrote: "It was also appropriate for us to provide, that as it is not permitted to any of the clerics to do penance,[103] thus also after penance and reconciliation it must not be permitted to any layman whomsoever to attain to the honor of the clerical

---

[101] This is a reference to Psalm 31:2: "Do not become like the horse and the mule, who have no understanding. With bit and bridle bind fast their jaws, who come not near unto thee."

[102] The 38th pope, who reigned from 384 to 399.

[103] The implication is not that clerics are exempt from penance, but rather that they are to be deprived of their clerical grade of order if they are to do penance.

office. For although they may be cleansed of all sin, those who were previously vessels of vices must not take up any of the instruments for conducting the sacraments."[104] Given, therefore, that Basil would instruct him who is guilty of this sin to undertake not only rigorous but also public penance, while Siricius prohibits the clerical orders from penance, it is obvious that he who has been polluted with the filthy baseness of lustful impurity with a male does not deserve to carry out ecclesiastical duties, nor is it fitting for those to handle the divine mystery,[105] who, so to speak, were previously vessels of vices.

[104] See the Epistles and Decrees of Pope St. Siricius, ep. 1, cap. 4 (PL 13, 1145).

[105] The word "mystery" in this context is a reference to the sacraments, and particularly the Eucharist. Thus, in the Roman Rite of the Catholic Church the Eucharist is referred to as the "Mystery of Faith."

XVII

THE PROPER CONDEMNATION
OF SODOMITIC INDECENCY

Certainly, this vice, which surpasses the savagery of all other vices, is to be compared to no other. For this vice is the death of bodies, the destruction of souls, pollutes the flesh, extinguishes the light of the intellect, expels the Holy Spirit from the temple of the human heart, introduces the diabolical inciter of lust, throws into confusion, and removes the truth completely from the deceived mind. It prepares snares for the one who walks, and for him who falls into the pit, it obstructs the escape. It opens up hell and closes the door of paradise. It makes the citizen of the heavenly Jerusalem into an heir of the Babylonian underworld. From the star of heaven, it produces the kindling of eternal fire. It cuts off a member of the Church and casts him into the voracious conflagration of raging Gehenna. This vice seeks to topple the walls of the heavenly homeland and busies itself with repairing the old walls of scorched Sodom. For it is this which violates sobriety, kills modesty, slays chastity. It butchers virginity with the sword of a most filthy contagion. It befouls everything, it stains everything, it pollutes everything, and for itself it permits nothing pure, nothing foreign to filth, nothing clean. For "all things," as the apostle states, "are clean to the clean: but to them that are defiled and to unbelievers, nothing is clean."[106]

---

[106] Titus 1:15.

This vice eliminates men from the choir of ecclesiastical assembly and compels them to pray with those who are possessed and oppressed by the devil.[107] It separates the soul from God, to unite it with demons. This most pestilent queen of the sodomites[108] renders him who is submissive to the laws of her tyranny indecent to men and hateful to God. In order to sow impious wars against God, she requires a militancy of the most wretched spirit. She separates the unhappy soul from the fellowship of the angels, removing it from its nobility to place it under the yoke of her own domination. She strips her soldiers of the armaments of the virtues, and to strike them down, exposes them to the darts of every vice. In the Church she humiliates, and in the forum she condemns. She defiles in secrecy and dishonors in public. She gnaws the conscience like worms, burns the flesh like a fire, and pants with desire for pleasure. But in contrast she fears to be exposed, to come out in public, to be known by others. For whom should he not fear, who also dreads the participant in common ruin with fearful suspicion, lest the same man who sins with him become judge of the crime by confession, when he might not hesitate not only to confess his sin but also to name the one with whom he sinned? Just as one could not die by sin without the other dying, so each one offers the other the occasion of rising again, when he rises.

His flesh burns with the fury of lust, his frigid mind trembles with the rancor of suspicion, and chaos now rages hellishly in the heart of the unhappy man while he is vexed by as many worries as he is tortured, as it were, by the torments of punishment. Indeed, once this most poisonous snake has

---

[107] This is a reference to canon 17 of the Council of Ancyra (see chapter 15).

[108] This is a reference to the vice of sodomy.

sunk its teeth into an unhappy soul, sense is immediately taken away, memory is removed, the sharpness of mind is obscured; it becomes forgetful of God, it forgets even itself. This plague removes the foundation of faith, enervates the strength of hope, breaks the tie of charity, destroys justice, undermines fortitude, banishes temperance, and blunts the sharpness of prudence. And what more shall I say? Since indeed it expels every cornerstone of the virtues from the court of the human heart, it also, as if the bolts of the doors have been removed, introduces every barbarity of the vices. To this, indeed, is appropriately applied the declaration of Jeremiah regarding the earthly Jerusalem: "The enemy," he says, "hath put out his hand to all her desirable things: for she hath seen the Gentiles enter into her sanctuary, of whom thou gavest commandment that they should not enter into thy church."[109]

Undoubtedly, whomever this most atrocious beast devours once with its cruel jaws, it binds from all good works and unleashes in every chasm of the most evil depravity. Whenever anyone falls into this abyss of most extreme perdition, he is exiled from the heavenly homeland, separated from the body of Christ, confounded by the authority of the whole Church, condemned by the judgment of all of the holy Fathers, despised among men on earth, and rejected from the fellowship of heavenly citizenry. Heaven is made for him like iron and earth like brass.[110] Neither there can he arise, weighted down by the gravity of his fault, nor here can he hide his evils any longer under the concealment of ignorance. He cannot here rejoice while he lives, nor there hope when he dies, because

---

[109] Lam.1:10.

[110] This is a reference to Lev. 26:19: "And I will break the pride of your stubbornness: and I will make to you the heaven above as iron, and the earth as brass."

he is forced now to bear the scorn of human derision, and then the torment of eternal damnation.

Indeed, that expression of prophetic lamentation is quite fitting for such a soul, which states, "Behold, O Lord, for I am in distress, my bowels are troubled: my heart is turned within me, for I am full of bitterness: abroad the sword destroyeth, and at home there is death alike."[111]

[111] Lam. 1:20.

XVIII

A WEEPING LAMENTATION OVER SOULS SURRENDERED TO THE DREGS OF IMPURITY

I myself, O unhappy soul, weep over you, and from the depths of my heart I sigh over your lot of perdition. I weep over you, I say, O miserable soul given over to the dregs of impurity, you who are to be lamented with a whole fountain of tears. For grief! "Who will give water to my head, and a fountain of tears to my eyes?"[112] And this doleful expression, now elicited from me in sobs, is no less suitable than when it was borne from the mouth of the prophet. For it is not the stony bulwark of a turreted city, not the overturned buildings of a temple made by hands that I bewail, nor do I lament the columns of common men led captive to the empire of the Babylonian king;[113] I mourn the noble soul, made in the image and likeness of God and united with the most precious blood of Christ, more glorious than many buildings, certainly to be preferred to all the pinnacles of earthly workmanship.

Therefore I lament the fall of the eminent soul and the destruction of the temple in which Christ had dwelt. May my eyes fail from weeping, may they pour out abundant streams of tears, and may they water sad and mournful expressions with continuous crying. May my eyes spring forth tears with the prophet day and night, and may they not cease "because

---

[112] Jer. 9:1.
[113] Cf. 2 Chron. 36.

the virgin daughter of my people is afflicted with a great af-
fliction, with a very sore plague, exceedingly."[114] Clearly the
daughter of my people has been crushed with the worst of
blows, because the soul, which had been the daughter of the
holy Church, has been cruelly injured with the dart of impurity by the enemy of the human race, and she who was once
tenderly and gently nurtured by the milk of sacred eloquence
in the palace of the eternal king, is now seen lying rigid and
swollen in the sulfurous embers of Gomorrah, pestilently
corrupted by the poison of lust. For "they that were fed del-
icately have died in the streets; they that were brought up in
scarlet have embraced the dung."[115]

Why? The prophet continues and says that it is because
"the iniquity of the daughter of my people is made greater
than the sin of Sodom, which was overthrown in a moment."[116] Indeed, the evil of the Christian soul surpasses the
sin of the Sodomites, because its sin is so much worse insofar
as it despises the mandates of evangelical grace, and, so that
it might not obtain the remedy of self-justifying subterfuge,
it is vehemently reprimanded by its own knowledge of the
divine law. Alas, alas, unhappy soul! Why do you not consider from what great height of dignity you must be cast,
of what grace of splendor and glory you must be stripped?
"How hath the Lord covered with obscurity the daughter of
Sion in his wrath!"[117] He has cast from heaven the glorious
one of Israel,[118] all splendor has gone out from the daugh-

---

[114] Jer. 14:17 (DR).

[115] Lam. 4:5.

[116] Lam. 4:6.

[117] Lam. 2:1.

[118] This is a paraphrasing of the second sentence of Lam. 2:1.

ter of Sion.[119] I, having compassion for your calamity, and most bitterly lamenting your disgrace, say, "Mine eyes have failed for tears, my bowels are troubled: my liver is poured out on the earth, for the destruction of the daughter of my people."[120] And you, failing to consider your evils and taking courage from your crime, say, "I sit a queen, and I am no widow!"[121] I proclaim your captivity with pity: "Why is Jacob commanded like a homeborn slave, and why has Israel become a prey?"[122] And you say, "I am rich and made wealthy and have need of nothing" and know not that "thou art wretched and miserable and poor and blind and naked."[123]

Consider, O wretched one, how much the darkness oppresses your soul. Take note how densely the fog of blindness envelops you. Has the fury of lust driven you towards the masculine sex? Has the madness of excess incited you to your own type; that is, man to man? Does a he-goat ever leap upon a he-goat, driven by lust? Does a ram jump upon a ram crazed by the ardor of sexual intercourse? A stallion gently and peacefully grazes in a single manger with another stallion, but having seen a mare, he is suddenly wild with the madness of desire. Never does a bull insolently approach another bull in sexual love, never does a male ass roar with a male ass in

[119] Cf. Lam. 1:6: "And from the daughter of Sion all her beauty is departed: her princes are become like rams that find no pastures."

[120] Lam. 2:11 (DR).

[121] See Rev. 18:7, regarding Babylon: "As much as she hath glorified herself and lived in delicacies, so much torment and sorrow give ye to her. Because she saith in her heart: I sit a queen and am no widow: and sorrow I shall not see."

[122] This is paraphrasing of Jer. 2:14: "Is Israel a bondman, or a homeborn slave? Why then is he become a prey?"

[123] Rev. 3:17.

copulation.[124] Therefore, degenerate men do not fear to perpetrate an act that even brute animals abhor. That which is done by the temerity of human depravity is condemned by the judgment of irrational cattle.

Speak, O emasculated man! Respond, O effeminate man! What do you seek in a man, that you are unable to find in yourself—what difference of sexes, what diverse features of members, what softness, what tenderness of carnal allurement, what pleasantness of a smooth face? The vigor of masculine appearance should frighten you, I entreat you, and your mind should abhor virile limbs. The purpose of the natural appetite is that each one seek externally what he is not able to find within the enclosure of his own means. If, therefore, the handling of masculine flesh delights you, turn your hands to yourself, and know that whatever you do not find in yourself, you seek in vain in another body.

Woe to you, unhappy soul, the destruction of which saddens the angels, and which enemies insult by applause! You have become the prey of demons, the plunder of the cruel, the booty of the impious: "All thy enemies have opened their mouth against thee: they have hissed, and gnashed with the teeth, and have said: We will swallow her up: lo, this is the day which we looked for: we have found it, we have seen it."[125]

---

[124] Researchers have recently documented species of animals in which some members engage in sexual behavior with same-sex partners. However, the phenomenon often, if not always, seems to be associated with a lack of availability of opposite-sex partners. See Jon Mooallem, "Can Animals be Gay?" *New York Times*, March 31, 2010, at www.nytimes.com.

[125] Lam. 2:16.

XIX

THAT THE SOUL SHOULD BE MOURNED, BECAUSE IT DOES NOT MOURN

Therefore I weep over you, O miserable soul, with so many lamentations, because I do not see you weeping. Therefore I lie prostrate on the ground on your behalf because I see you wickedly upright following such a grave fall, even wantonly striving towards the pinnacle of ecclesiastical order. Otherwise, if you had lowered yourself in humility, I, sure of your restoration, would have exulted in the Lord with all that is in me; if the worthy compunction of a contrite heart had shaken the hidden recesses of your soul, I would have rightly taken delight with a dance of ineffable joy.

You are most greatly to be wept over, because you do not weep. You are in need of the sufferings of others because you do not feel the danger of your ruin, and you are to be wept over all the more by bitter tears of fraternal compassion because you are not troubled by your own sorrowful lamentation. Why do you neglect to consider the weight of your condemnation? Why do you not cease to store up wrath for yourself on the day of judgment[126] by first submerging yourself in the depths of sin and then raising yourself up in arrogance? That curse is coming, is coming upon you, which was cast by the mouth of David against Joab and his house following the spilling of the blood of Abner. That pestilence

---

[126] Rom. 2:5.

of Gomorrah, which doomed the house of Joab in retribution of cruel homicide, now lives in the habitation of your body.[127]

After Abner is struck down, David says: "I, and my kingdom are innocent … forever of the blood of Abner the son of Ner: and may it come upon the head of Joab, and upon all his father's house: and let there not fail from the house of Joab one that bears Gomorrah."[128] For which a second translation reads: "… that hath an issue of seed, and that is a leper holding the distaff,[129] and that falleth by the sword, and that wanteth bread." For he who is befouled by the stain of grave sin is sprinkled with leprosy. To hold a distaff, in fact, is to abandon the manly activity of a masculine life and to exhibit the alluring softness of feminine manners. He who falls by the sword is one who incurs the fury of divine indignation. He who is lacking in bread is restricted from the reception of the body of Christ by the penalty of his particular offense, for "this is the living bread that came down from heaven."[130]

[127] Abner was the general of the army of the Israelite king Saul, who made peace with Saul's rival and successor, David, but was later murdered by Joab, an ally of David, over a personal dispute. David uttered a bitter curse against Joab and his whole family for this crime. See 2 Sam. 2–3.

[128] 2 Sam. 3:28–29 (2 Kings in the Vulgate/Douay schema). As Damian proceeds to note, this is one of two translations available to him, which ends with the phrase *Gomorrhianum sustinens* ("bearing Gomorrah") in contrast with the Clementine Vulgate (see following footnote). The words "before the Lord" following the word "innocent" are omitted in Damian's quotation, and I have thus marked it with an ellipsis.

[129] This "second translation" is virtually identical to the Clementine Vulgate. I am unable to find examples of the first. Here "distaff" is a translation of the Latin word *fusus*, which may also mean "spindle." As Damian observes, the distaff is often associated with femininity in classical literature.

[130] Cf. John 6:59: "This is the bread that came down from heaven" and John 6:51 "I am the living bread which came down from heaven."

So if, O unworthy priest, you will be compelled by precept of law to remain outside the encampments after the leprous flow of semen is completed, why do you still strive to obtain even the preeminence of honor in those same encampments? Is it not true that Ozias the king, when he had haughtily wished to burn incense over the altar of incense, afterwards recognized that he had been struck by heaven with the disease of leprosy, and not only patiently accepted his expulsion from the temple by the priests, but rather himself made haste to quickly leave? Indeed it is written: "And when Azarias the priest looked upon him, and all of the remaining priests, they saw the leprosy on his forehead, and they quickly expelled him," and then the following is added: "Yea himself also being frightened, hasted to go out, because he had quickly felt the stroke of the Lord."[131]

If the king, having been struck with corporeal leprosy, did not despise to be ejected from the temple by the priests, why do you, who are leprous in your soul, not suffer yourselves to be removed from the sacred altars in accordance with the judgment of so many of the holy Fathers? If he, having lost the authority of royal dignity, did not blush to live in an ordinary house until his death, why are you troubled about descending from the height of the sacerdotal office so that, enclosed in the tomb of penance as if dead, you might strive to join the ranks of the living? And, so that we might return to that mystical story of Joab, if you yourself fell by the sword, how will you raise another by priestly grace? If you are deservedly lacking bread—that is, you are separated from Christ in your body— how will you be able to satisfy another with the banquet of the celestial table? If you are struck on your forehead with the leprosy of Ozias—that is, if you are disgraced by the sign of

[131] Chron. 26:20.

dishonor on your face—how will you be able to wash another clean of a perpetrated offense?

May bloated pride blush, therefore, and not vainly seek to be raised above itself, as it weighs well below itself by the burden of its own guilt. May it learn to ponder its evils with subtle consideration, may it learn to contain itself humbly within its own limits, lest it arrogantly usurp that which it cannot obtain in any way and entirely lose even that for which true humility might have been able to hope.

XX

THAT THE SERVICE OF AN UNWORTHY PRIEST IS THE RUIN OF THE PEOPLE

Why, I ask, O damnable sodomites, do you seek after the height of ecclesiastical dignity with such burning ambition? Why do you seek with such longing to snare the people of God in the web of your perdition? Does it not suffice for you that you cast your very selves off the high precipice of villainy, unless you also involve others in the danger of your fall?

If perchance someone comes to urge us to intercede on his behalf with some powerful man who is angry with him, but who is unknown to us, we should immediately respond that we cannot come to intercede, because we do not know him personally. If, therefore, one blushes to intercede with a man of whom he can presume nothing, by what reasoning does a man who does not know himself to be an intimate of the grace of God through a meritorious life, take up the duty of intercession with God on behalf of the people? How does he plead for pardon from God on behalf of others, if he doesn't know if God is well disposed to him? Regarding which there is something else to be feared more anxiously: that he who is believed to be able to placate wrath might deserve this same wrath due to his own guilt. For all of us clearly know that when one who is displeasing is sent to intercede, he further provokes the one who is already annoyed.

He, therefore, who is still held bound by terrestrial desires, should beware, lest, stoking ever more the ire of the strict

Judge while he delights in his glorious position, he might become the cause of ruin to his subjects. Each one, therefore, should take wise measure of himself, lest he dare to act as a priest while vice continues to reign damnably within him, lest he, depraved by his own offense, seek to become an intercessor for the sins of others. Forbear therefore, forbear, and beware of inextinguishably inflaming the fury of God against you, lest by your prayers you more sharply provoke Him whom you patently offend by your evil acts, and while your ruin is certain, beware of being made guilty of the ruin of another. For the less you fall by sinning, the more easily you may rise again by the outstretched hand of penance, through the mercy of God.

XXI

THAT GOD DOES NOT WISH TO RECEIVE SACRIFICE FROM THE HANDS OF THE IMPURE[132]

If the omnipotent God himself disdains to accept sacrifice from your hands, who are you, who presume to importunately thrust it upon Him who does not wish it? For the sacrifices of the impious are abominable to God.[133] But to those among you who are angry with me and refuse to listen to the writer, at least listen to the one who speaks to you from the prophetic mouth. Listen to him, I say, declaring, thundering, rejecting your sacrifices, publicly denouncing your services. For Isaiah, select among the prophets—indeed, the Holy Spirit by the mouth of Isaiah—says:

> Hear the word of the Lord, ye rulers of Sodom, give ear to the law of our God, ye people of Gomorrah. To what purpose do you offer me the multitude of your victims, saith the Lord? I am full, I have not desired holocausts of rams, and fat of fatlings, and blood of calves, and lambs, and buck goats. When you came to appear before me, who required these things at your hands, that you should walk in my courts? Offer sacrifice no more in vain: incense is

[132] Damian does not here argue that the sacrifice of the Mass, the principle act of worship in the Catholic Church, is sacramentally invalid when offered by a priest who is soiled by grave sin, but rather that it is a sin for a priest to offer the sacrifice in such a state. See Translator's Preface for details.

[133] Cf. Prov. 15:8; 21:27.

an abomination to me. The new moons, and the Sabbaths, and other festivals I will not abide, your assemblies are wicked. My soul hateth your new moons, and your solemnities: they are become troublesome to me, I am weary of bearing them. And when you stretch forth your hands, I will turn away my eyes from you: and when you multiply prayer, I will not hear ... your hands are full of blood.[134]

Observe, therefore, that although the sentence of divine punishment must strike all of the evils of the vices in common, it is hurled chiefly upon the princes of the Sodomites and the people of Gomorrah, so that even if the temerity of the contentious refuses to believe human testimony regarding the nature of this mortal vice, it might at least acquiesce to divine testimony. However, if someone objects that the following is added to the prophetic statement, "Your hands are full of blood"—so that in this declaration of divine invective he wishes homicide, rather than carnal impurity, to be understood—he will discover in the divine utterances that all sins are called "blood." To this David attests, saying, "Deliver me from bloods, O God."[135] Yet if we also seek to carefully examine the nature of this vice and to recall to mind the maxims of the natural philosophers, we find that the flow of semen is generated from blood. For as by the agitation of the winds the water of the sea is converted into foam, so by the touching of the genitals, blood is made into semen by excitation.

Therefore, one is not far from a proper understanding if one interprets "your hands are full of blood" as meaning

---

[134] Isa. 1:10–15. This translation is taken from the DRC, except the phrase "I have desired not" which is rendered there in the present tense. The word "for," which is in the Clementine Vulgate, is omitted in Damian's text, where I have placed an ellipsis.

[135] Ps. 50:16 (DR).

the pestilence of impurity. And perhaps this was because the vengeance against Joab proceeded from none other than the guilt of spilled blood, so that he who had willfully spilled the blood of another would be struck with a worthy punishment if he suffered unwillingly the outflowing of his own blood.[136] But as we have arrived, through a long disputation, at the point of clearly showing the Lord himself reprobating and resoundingly prohibiting the sacrifices of those who are unclean, why are we sinners surprised if we are scorned by such people for our admonitions? If we note that the authority of divine utterance is little heeded by the hardened heart of the reprobate, is it any wonder if we, who are on earth, are not believed?

---

[136] That is, the perverse spilling of his semen, per Damian's interpretation of 1 Sam. 3, explained in chapter 19.

XXII

THAT NO HOLY OFFERING IS RECEIVED BY GOD IF IT IS STAINED BY THE FILTH OF IMPURITY

So now, he who disdains the venerable councils of the holy Fathers, who despises the precepts of the apostles and of apostolic men, who has not feared to disregard the edicts of canonical punishment, and who thinks little of the rule of divine authority itself, is at least to be admonished to place the day of his summons before his eyes, and should not doubt that the more he sins, the more harshly he will he be judged. As is said by the angel using the metaphor of Babylon, "As much as she hath glorified herself and lived in delicacies, so much torment and sorrow give ye to her."[137]

He should be admonished to consider that, however long he does not cease to suffer from the malady of this vice, even if he is acknowledged as having done some good, he does not deserve to receive a reward. No religiosity, no self-mortification, no perfection of life which is soiled by such filthy impurity will be deemed worthy in the eyes of the celestial Judge. However, to prove that these things are true, let the testimony of the venerable Bede[138] be presented:

---

[137] Rev. 18:7.

[138] Damian's source erroneously attributes the following quotation to the Venerable Bede, when in fact it is a maxim of Pope St. Gregory the Great followed by a commentary originating in the 10th century (see Translator's Preface and footnote below).

He who thus gives alms while not discharging his guilt, does not redeem his soul which he does not restrain from vices. This is demonstrated by the actions of that hermit who, having many virtues, had entered into the eremitic life[139] with a certain associate of his. The thought was injected into him by the devil that whenever his sexual passions were excited he should discharge his semen by the rubbing of his genital member, just as he might expel mucus from the nostrils. For this reason, as he died he was turned over to demons while his companion watched. Then the same companion, who was ignorant of his guilt, and recalling his virtuous exercises, almost despaired, saying, "Who can be saved, if this man has perished?" Then an angel standing by said to him, "Do not be troubled, for this man, although he might have accomplished much, has nonetheless soiled everything by that vice which the apostle[140] calls 'impurity.'"[141]

[139] The Latin here reads simply *deservisset*, which means, "had deserted" or "had gone out," which is a shorthand expression referring to the desertion of the world in favor of the life of a hermit.

[140] That is, St. Paul (Rom. 1:24).

[141] Rather than the Venerable Bede, the first sentence of this quotation is a paraphrasing of Pope St. Gregory the Great (*Moralia in Iob*, lib. 12; PL 75, 1013). The rest of the quotation, which seeks to illustrate this precept of Gregory, appears to originate in the 10th century in the *Collationes* of St. Odo, abbot of Cluny (see PL 133, 570C–D), as well as in *De Corpore et Sanguine Christi*, cap. 60 (PL 137, 403A), a work of Odo's contemporary, the Italian bishop Gezo of Tortona, who conflates the Pope Gregory quotation with Odo's commentary and gives no attribution. It seems probable that one of Damian's reference works replicated the quotation from Gezo's work and attached an incorrect attribution to Bede. See Translator's Preface for details.

XXIII

THAT ALL OF THE ABOVE-NAMED FORMS CONSTITUTE SODOMY

Therefore, no one should flatter himself that he has not fallen with someone else if he slips into these defilements of sensual enticement by himself, as that unhappy hermit who is turned over to demons at the moment of death should be understood not to have polluted another, but to have ruined himself by defilement. Just as from one planting of a vine various shoots spring forth, so from one sodomitic impurity, as a most poisonous root, those four growths enumerated above rise up,[142] so that whoever might pick the pestilential grapes from any one of them likewise perishes, immediately infected with the poison.

For their vine is from the vineyard of the Sodomites, and their offshoots are from Gomorrah. "Their grapes are grapes of gall, and their clusters most bitter."[143] For this serpent, which we labor to crush with the stake of our argument, has four heads, and he injects all of the poison of his wickedness with the tooth of whichever head has bitten. Therefore, whether one pollutes only himself, or another by fondling him with his hands, or copulating between the thighs, or even

---

[142] That is, the four grades of the sin of sodomy laid out by Damian in chapter one.

[143] Deut. 32:32.

violating him in the rear, regardless of such distinctions[144] he is without a doubt guilty of having committed a sodomitic offense. For we do not read that those residents of Sodom only fell into the rear ends of others, but rather it is to be believed that, following the impulse of unrestrained lust, they carried out their indecencies in various ways on themselves or on others.

Clearly if some place of indulgence were to be provided in the ruin of this vice, to whom would forgiveness be more applicable than to that hermit, who sinned without knowing, who fell in the ignorance of his simplicity, who concluded that it was permitted to him as a duty of natural obligation? May such wretched people learn, may they learn to restrain themselves from the pestilence of such a detestable vice, to manfully overcome the alluring lasciviousness of sexual desire, to repress the wanton incitement of the flesh, to fear deeply the terrible sentence of divine punishment, ever calling to mind that maxim of apostolic admonition, which states, "It is a fearful thing to fall into the hands of the living God."[145] They should also recall that which the prophet menacingly cries out, saying that in the fire of the zeal of the Lord all the earth will be devoured,[146] and all flesh in his sword.[147]

For if carnal men are to be devoured by the divine sword, why do they now damnably love the same flesh? Why do they weakly cede to the pleasures of the flesh? It is undoubtedly

[144] The Latin phrase here is *licet discretione servata*, which is literally "although discretion/distinction is maintained."

[145] Heb. 10:31.

[146] Cf. Zeph. 1:18: "In the fire of his jealousy shall the earth be devoured, because he will make consummation with speed to all that inhabit the earth" (DR).

[147] Cf. Isa. 66:16: "For the Lord shall judge by fire, and by his sword unto all flesh, and the slain of the Lord shall be many ..."

that sword, which the Lord through Moses points at sinners, saying, "I shall whet my sword as the lightning,"[148] and again, "My sword shall devour flesh"[149]—that is, my fury will swallow those who live in the delight of the flesh. For just as those who fight against the abominations of the vices are supported by the help of heavenly virtue, so those who, to the contrary, are given to the impurity of the flesh, are reserved for the sole sentence of divine vengeance. Thus Peter also says, "The Lord knoweth how to deliver the godly from temptation, but to reserve the unjust unto the day of judgment to be tormented: and especially them who walk after the flesh in the lust of uncleanness."[150] And scolding them elsewhere, he says, "… counting for a pleasure the delights of a day: stains and spots, sporting themselves to excess, rioting in their feasts with you: having eyes full of adultery and of sin that ceaseth not."[151]

Those who have been placed in holy orders should not glory if they live detestably, because the higher they stand, the further they fall, and because they should now excel others in a life of holy conversation, they will later be required to endure more severe punishments. As Peter states, "For if God spared not the angels that sinned, but delivered them, drawn down by infernal ropes to the lower hell, unto torments, to be reserved unto judgment…. And reducing the cities of the Sodomites and of the Gomorrhites into ashes, condemned

---

[148] Deut. 32:41.

[149] Deut. 32:42.

[150] 2 Pet. 2:9–10.

[151] 2 Pet. 2:13–14. In this quotation, the genitive of "day" *(diei)* was rendered incorrectly in medieval manuscripts as *Dei* (the genitive form of "God"), and the nominative plural of "spots" *(coinquinationes)* as the genitive singular *coinquinationis*. In addition, the word "their" *(suis)* is omitted. The Gaetani edition corrects these errors.

them to be overthrown, making them an example to those that should after act wickedly."[152] Why does the holy apostle turn to the destruction of Sodom and Gomorrah after relating the fall of diabolical damnation, unless it is to clearly show that those who are now given to the vice of impurity will be damned to eternal punishment along with the unclean spirits, and that those who are now vexed by the ardor of sodomitic lust must later burn in the flame of perpetual combustion with the very author of all iniquity?

The apostle Jude most appropriately agrees with this view as well, saying, "The angels who kept not their principality but forsook their own habitation, he hath reserved under darkness in everlasting chains, unto the judgment of the great day. As Sodom and Gomorrah and the neighbouring cities, in like manner, having given themselves to fornication and going after other flesh, were made an example, suffering the punishment of eternal fire."[153] It is therefore clear, that just as the angels who do not recognize their superior position deserve to suffer in the darkness of the underworld, so also those who fall from the dignity of holy orders into the chasm of sodomy, are rightly plunged into the abyss of perpetual damnation.

To briefly conclude, whoever has soiled himself with the contamination of sodomitic disgrace, in whatever way distinguished above, unless he is cleansed by the fulfillment of fruitful penance, can never have the grace of God, will never be worthy of the body and blood of Christ, and will never cross the threshold of the celestial homeland, as is manifestly declared in the Book of Revelation by the apostle John, who, while speaking of the glory of the heavenly kingdom, adds:

[152] 2 Pet. 2:4, 6.
[153] Jude 6–7.

"There shall not enter into it anyone defiled and that worketh abomination."[154]

---

[154] Cf. Rev. 21:27. The Clementine Vulgate has "anything" *(aliquod)* rather than Damian's "anyone" *(aliquis)*.

XXIV

AN EXHORTATION TO THE MAN
WHO HAS FALLEN INTO SIN,
THAT HE MIGHT RISE AGAIN

Arise, arise, I implore you! Wake up O man who sinks in the sleep of wretched pleasure! Revive at last, you who have fallen by the lethal sword before the face of your enemies! The apostle Paul is here! Hear him, hear him proclaiming, urging, rousing, crying out to you with clear maxims: "Rise, thou that sleepest, and arise from the dead: and Christ shall awaken thee."[155]

You who hear Christ the reviver, why do you despair of your own resuscitation? Hear it from his own mouth: "He that believeth in me, although he be dead, shall live."[156] If Life the vivifier wishes to raise you up, why do you bear to continue lying in your death?[157] Beware then, beware, lest the abyss of despair swallow you up. May your soul faithfully trust in divine kindness, lest it become hardened in impenitence by the magnitude of the crime. For it is not sinners who despair, but the impious,[158] nor is it the magnitude of offenses that leads the soul into despair, but rather impiety. For if only the

[155] Cf. Eph. 5:14. Where the Clementine Vulgate has *lluminabit* (enlighten) Damian's version has *exsuscitabit* (awaken).

[156] John 11:25.

[157] That is, Jesus Christ, who is "the way, the truth, and the life" (John 14:6).

[158] That is, it is not mere sinners who despair, but those impious who do not trust in the mercy of God.

devil was able to submerge you in the depths of this vice, how much more is the strength of Christ able to return you to that pinnacle from which you fell? Shall he that fell rise again no more?[159]

The ass of your flesh,[160] under the weight of a burden, has fallen into the mud; it is the spur to penance which pricks, it is the hand of the Spirit, which vigorously extracts it. That most strong Samson, because he wrongly disclosed the secret of his heart to a coaxing woman, not only lost seven strands of hair by which his strength was maintained, but also, after being captured by the Philistines, lost his eyes. However, after his hairs had regrown, he humbly requested the help of the Lord God, leveled the temple of Dagon, and annihilated a much greater number of the enemy than he had before.[161]

Therefore, if your unchaste flesh has deceived you by enticing you to pleasures, if it has taken away the seven gifts of the Holy Spirit, [162] if it has extinguished the light not of the countenance, but of the heart, do not falter in your courage, do not despair utterly; continue to gather your strength, strive manfully, dare to attempt the courageous, and you will be able to triumph, by the mercy of God, over your enemies. The Philistines certainly were able to shave the hair of Samson, but not to uproot it, and so although evil spirits have excluded the charisms of the Holy Spirit from you for a while, by no

---

[159] Cf. Ps. 40:9 (Vulgate/Douay numbering): "Shall he that sleepeth rise again no more?" A similar phrase also appears in Jeremiah 8:4: "Shall not he that falleth, rise again?"

[160] The body portrayed as a stubborn ass was also a theme of St. Francis of Assisi, who referred to his body as "brother ass" (see Francis biographer Thomas of Celano, *Vita Secunda*, 82).

[161] See Judg. 16.

[162] Enumerated in Isaiah 11:2.

means are they able to irrecoverably deny the remedy of divine reconciliation.

How, I ask, are you able to despair of the abundant mercy of the Lord, who even rebuked Pharaoh for not fleeing to the remedy of penance after sinning? Hearken to what he says: "I have crushed the arms of Pharaoh, king of Egypt, and he has not asked to be given health, and for strength to be returned to him for grasping the sword."[163] What ought I say of Achab, the king of Israel? After he constructed idols, after he impiously slaughtered Naboth the Jezrahelite, he was finally partially humiliated and also partially found mercy. For, according to the Scripture, after receiving the terror of divine warning, "he rent his garments, and put haircloth upon his flesh, and fasted and slept in sackcloth, and walked with his head cast down."[164]

What followed? "The word of the Lord came to Elias, the Thesbite, saying: Hast thou not seen Achab humbled before me? Therefore, because he hath humbled himself for my sake, I will not bring the evil in his days."[165] Therefore, if the penance of that man who is known to have persevered is not despised, why do you despair of the abundance of the divine

[163] Cf. Ezek. 30:21. The quotation differs substantially from that found in the Clementine Vulgate: "Son of man, I have broken the arm of Pharaoh king of Egypt: and behold it is not bound up, to be healed, to be tied up with clothes, and swathed with linen, that it might recover strength, and hold the sword." The Latin quoted by Damian, which seems to be an interpretation of the passage, appears verbatim in a letter of Bachiarius of Spain, an early fifth century ecclesiastical writer (*De Reparatione Lapsi*, cap. 11; PL 20, 1048A). It also appears in Burchard's *Libri Decretorum*, lib. 19, cap. 48 (PL 140, 994C), where it erroneously attributed to a letter of St. John Chrysostom to Theodore of Mopsuestia. This is most probably Damian's source. See Translator's Preface for details.

[164] 3 Kings 21:27.

[165] 3 Kings 21:28–29.

mercy, if you indefatigably strive to persevere? Enter into a constant struggle with the flesh, and always stand armed against the importunate fury of lust. If the flame of wantonness burns in your bones, the recollection of perpetual fire should immediately extinguish it. If the clever deceiver presents you with the sleek beauty of the flesh, your mind should immediately turn its eye to the graves of the dead and carefully note what there is agreeable to touch or delightful to see. It should thus consider that the slime that now stinks intolerably, that the pus that gives birth to worms and feeds them, that whatever dust, whatever dry ashes are seen there to lie, were once joyful flesh that was subject to passions of this kind during its youth. Finally, it should imagine the rigid tendons, the bare teeth, the separated structure of bones and joints, and the whole composition of members chaotically dispersed. A monster of such terrible deformity and jumbled likeness expels illusion from the human heart.

Consider, therefore, how perilous is the exchange: for a momentary pleasure, in which semen is ejected in an instant, the punishment that follows does not end for thousands of years! Consider how wretched it is that, for the sake of one member whose enjoyment is now fulfilled, the whole body together with the soul is perpetually tormented by the most dreadful conflagration of flames! Repulse such imminent evils with the impenetrable shields of this thought and others of the same kind, and eliminate those of the past through penance. Let fasting break the arrogance of the flesh, and let the soul be enlarged, fattened by feasts of prayer. In this way, the presiding spirit may restrain the subjected flesh by the bridle of discipline and strive daily to hasten to the heavenly Jerusalem by steps of fervent desire.

XXV

THAT FOR THE TAMING OF SEXUAL DESIRE, IT SHOULD BE SUFFICIENT TO CONTEMPLATE THE REWARDS OF CHASTITY

In work there is also recompense, so you should incessantly consider the promised rewards of chastity, and roused by their sweetness, pass over any opposing scheme of the clever entrapper with the unimpeded foot of faith. For if one meditates on the happiness that is not obtained without toil, the labor is easily carried out, and the hired laborer lightens the tedium of work while eagerly anticipating the earnings that are owed to him.

Consider, therefore, what is said of the soldiers of chastity by the prophet: "Thus saith our Lord to the eunuchs: They that shall keep my sabbaths, and shall choose the things that I would, and shall hold my covenant, I will give unto them in my house and within my walls a place, and a name better than sons and daughters."[166] Indeed, eunuchs are those who repress the insolent impulses of the flesh and cut away from themselves the performance of perverse acts.[167] However, most of those who are devoted to the pleasure of carnal attraction long to leave behind themselves a memory of their name through the posterity of descendants. This they desire with all

---

[166] Isa. 56:4–5 (DR).

[167] The expression "cut away" here uses castration as a metaphor for voluntary celibacy.

their heart, because by no means do they regard themselves as dying completely to this world if they perpetuate the glory of their name through the surviving bud of descendants who remain. But much more gloriously and much more happily do the celibate accept the same office for which the common man is inflamed by such passions of fervent ambition, because their memory always lives with Him who is eternal, and not subject to temporal law. Therefore, by divine declaration, a name better than that of sons and daughters is promised to the eunuchs, because they deserve to possess in perpetuity, without any hindrance of oblivion, the memory of a name that the posterity of children would have been able to extend through a brief space of time. For "the just shall be in everlasting remembrance."[168]

In the Book of Revelation it is also said through John, "And they shall walk with me in white, because they are worthy … and I will not blot out their name out of the book of life,"[169] and there again it is said, "These are they which are not defiled with women. For they are virgins. These follow the Lamb whithersoever he shall go,"[170] and what song they sing, no one can say, except that 144,000.[171] Indeed, the virgins sing that special song to the Lamb because they perpetually exult with him over the incorruption of the flesh[172] before all the faithful. Clearly, others among the just cannot sing the same song, although those having the same beatitude might deserve

[168] Ps. 111:7 (Vulgate/Douay numbering).

[169] Rev. 3:4–5.

[170] Rev. 14:4 (DR).

[171] See Rev. 14:3: "And they sung as it were a new canticle, before the throne and before the four living creatures and the ancients: and no man could say the canticle, but those hundred forty-four thousand who were purchased from the earth."

[172] That is, the purity of celibacy.

to hear it, because in charity they indeed look joyfully upon their high position, yet do not rise to the level of their reward. For this reason it is to be considered and reconsidered in our mind with all zeal, how dignified and how excellent it is to be elevated to the summit of that place where it is perfect happiness to be among even the lowest; there the exalted in privilege ascend, where it is most blessed to preserve the equal rights of equity.[173] Doubtlessly, as the Truth testifies, not everyone takes this proverb in this generation,[174] and thus not all ultimately arrive at that glory of exceptional reward.

These things, and many others of this kind, beloved brother, whoever you are, consider in the hidden places of your soul, and with all strength make haste to keep your flesh pure from all pestilence of lust, so that, in accordance with the decree of apostolic doctrine, you might know how to possess your vessel "in sanctification and honor, not in the passion of lust, like the Gentiles that know not God."[175] If you still stand, beware the precipices, but if you have slipped, faithfully extend your hand to the hook of penance which is available everywhere, so that you who were not able to live far from Sodom with Abraham, may be able to emigrate with Lot, even as the fiery destruction is already urging. For you who had

[173] The phrase, "to preserve the equal (or proportional) rights of equity," *(paria equitatis iura servare)* appears to be a reference to the medieval legal dictum "equity requires equal laws for equal cases" *(aequitas in paribus casis paria iura desiderat)*.

[174] Cf. Christ's words regarding the renunciation of marriage: "All men take not this word, but they to whom it is given. For there are eunuchs, who were born so from their mothers' womb: and there are eunuchs, who were made so by men: and there are eunuchs, who have made themselves eunuchs for the kingdom of heaven. He that can take, let him take it" (Matt. 19:11–12).

[175] 1 Thess. 4:4–5.

not been able to enter the port, may it at least suffice to have avoided shipwreck from the wave you endured, and may it be pleasing to you who have not merited to arrive in the bay without loss, having disembarked upon the sands following the danger, to sing the song of the blessed Jonah in a cheerful voice: "All thy billows, and thy waves passed over me. And I said: I am cast away out of the sight of thy eyes: but yet I shall see thy holy temple again."[176]

[176] Jon. 2:4–5.

XXVI

WHERE THE WRITER DEFENDS HIMSELF HONORABLY

If, however, this little book might have reached the hands of anyone whose conscience cannot at all bear what is written above, and is by chance displeased by it, and accuses me of being a traitor and an informer of the crimes of my brothers, he should know that I have sought with all zeal the favor of the interior Judge, but do not fear the hatred of the depraved or the tongues of detractors. Indeed, I prefer to be thrown innocent into a well with Joseph,[177] who accused his brothers of the worst of crimes to their father, than to be punished by the retribution of divine fury with Eli, who saw the evil of his children and was silent.[178]

For, knowing that the divine voice threatens frighteningly by the mouth of the prophet saying, "If you see your brother doing evil, and you do not correct him, I will require his blood from your hand,"[179] who am I to watch such a noxious

---

[177] That is, Joseph, the son of Jacob, grandson of Abraham. See Gen. 37.

[178] That is, the high priest Eli, who rebuked but did not discipline his sons when they engaged in abuses of the priestly office. As a punishment, Eli's children were killed in battle, and the Ark of the Covenant, which contained the stone tablets upon which the Ten Commandments had been inscribed, was temporarily lost to Israel's enemies. Eli himself died upon receiving the news. See 1 Sam. 2; 4.

[179] This is a paraphrase of Ez. 3:18: "If, when I say to the wicked, Thou shalt surely die: thou declare it not to him, nor speak to him, that he may be converted from his wicked way, and live: the same wicked

crime spreading among those in holy orders and keeping silent, to dare to await the accounting of divine punishment as the murderer of another's soul, and to begin to be made a debtor of that guilt of which I had been by no means the author? Moreover, while the Scripture says, "Cursed be he that withholdeth his sword from blood," [180] you urge me to place the sword of my tongue in a sheath of silence, so that it itself might perish while it rusts in disfavor, and be of no use to others while it does not pierce the faults of those who live depraved lives!

Indeed, to prohibit the sword from blood is to restrain the word of correction from striking carnal ways of life. Of which sword again it is said, "From his mouth came out a sharp two-edged sword."[181] For how am I loving my neighbor as myself, if I negligently allow the wound, by which I do not doubt him to be dying a cruel death, to fester in his soul? Seeing therefore the spiritual wounds, should I neglect to cure them by the surgery of words? The eminent preacher who believes himself to be clean of the blood of others insofar as he does not refrain from punishing their vices, does not teach me thus. For he says, "Wherefore I take you to witness this day that I am clear from the blood of all men. For I have not spared to declare unto you all the counsel of God."[182] I am not so instructed by John, who is instructed by the angelic

---

man shall die in his iniquity, but I will require his blood at thy hand," and 3:20: "Moreover if the just man shall turn away from his justice, and shall commit iniquity: I will lay a stumblingblock before him, he shall die, because thou hast not given him warning: he shall die in his sin, and his justices which he hath done, shall not be remembered: but I will require his blood at thy hand."

[180] Jer. 48:10.

[181] Rev. 1:16.

[182] Acts 20: 26–27.

admonition, "He that heareth, let him say: Come"[183]—indeed, so that he who receives the interior call might bring others with him by also crying out, lest even he who is called find the doors closed if he approaches alone the one who calls him.

If you think that it is right to rebuke me who rebukes, and, so to speak, to accuse me of presumptuous accusation, why do you not reproach Jerome, who disputes so caustically against various sects of heretics? Why do you not censure Ambrose, who preaches publicly against the Arians, and why not Augustine, the severe disputant who inveighs against the Manicheans and the Donatists?[184] You say to me, "They acted rightly, because they reviled heretics and blasphemers, but you do not fear to do the same to Christians." To which I briefly respond: just as they struggled to return to the flock those who had left and were lost, so it is also our intention to prevent the exit of those who in some way remain inside. They once said, "They went out from us, but they were not of us. For if they had been of us, they would no doubt have remained with us."[185] And we say, "They indeed are with us, but in a bad way. Therefore let us strive, if it be possible, that hereafter they might be with us in a good way."

This also we add, that if the worst sin is blasphemy, I do not know in what sense sodomy is better.[186] For the former causes men to stray, the latter, to perish. The former separates

[183] Rev. 22:17.

[184] St. Jerome, St. Ambrose, and St. Augustine, are three of the four original Doctors of the Latin Church who are eminent for their teaching, the fourth being Pope St. Gregory the Great.

[185] 1 John 2:19.

[186] Damian's use of "we" at the beginning of the sentence seems to be carried over from the analogy he draws in the previous paragraph, in which the apostle John speaks of "us." Damian here shifts to "I" to indicate that the statement following is his own.

the soul from God; the latter joins it to the devil. The former expels it from paradise; the latter plunges it into Tartarus.[187] The former blinds the eyes of discernment; the latter casts into an abyss of ruin. And if we take care to investigate with precision which of the two crimes weighs more heavily on the scale of divine judgment, the Sacred Scripture, having been consulted, more clearly teaches us. There the children of Israel, who blaspheme God by worshipping idols, are lead into captivity, but the Sodomites are found to have been devoured in the flames of heavenly fire and sulfur.

I have not presented the holy doctors so that I might presume to compare the smoking firebrand to the bright stars—I indeed who am hardly able to commemorate such excellent men with my unworthy mouth without committing an offense! However, I say that what they have done by reproaching and confounding vices, they have also taught their inferiors to do, and if in their time this plague had arisen with such liberty of impudence, we believe without a doubt that copious volumes of books written against it would be seen today. Therefore, no one should judge me for arguing against a mortal vice, given that I do not seek opprobrium, but rather the advancement of fraternal well-being—otherwise, while persecuting the one who rebukes, one might seem to favor the offender.

To use the words of Moses, "If any man be on the Lord's side, let him join with me."[188] That is to say that anyone who considers himself to be a soldier of God should fervently gird himself to confound this vice, should not cease to fight it with all of his strength, and should endeavor to run it through and destroy it with the sharpest darts of words, wherever it might be found. So when the captor is engulfed by a thick array of

---

[187] That is, hell.
[188] Ex. 32:26.

troops, the captive might be freed from those fetters with which he had been enslaved, and when all unanimously cry out in one consonant voice against the tyrant, he who was being carried away is immediately ashamed of being made the prize of the raging monster. He who does not doubt, by the testimony of many bearing witness, that he is being carried away to death, should not be slow to return to life as soon as possible after coming to his senses.[189]

---

[189] Literally, "having returned to himself" *(in semetipsum reversus)*.

XXVII

WHERE A STATEMENT IS ADDRESSED
TO THE LORD POPE

Now to you, most blessed pope, we return at the end of this little work. To you we recall the point of our pen, so that the ending of the work that has been carried out might be rightly completed for him to whom the beginning is directed. We therefore request and humbly implore that your clemency, if it is right to say so, carefully examine the decrees of the sacred canons, which are already well known to you, and that you designate spiritual and prudent men for this necessary investigation, so you might respond to us regarding these chapters in order to remove every scruple of doubt from our heart.

Nor do we thus presume to say this as if we do not know how to apply to this matter the expertise of your profundity alone, which has God as its author, but so that when the testimony of sacred authority is applied, when the matter is resolved by the consensus and judgment of many, the accusations of perverse men, which perhaps they would not have blushed to mutter in opposition, might be laid to rest. For what is established by the judgment of many is not easy to dispute. However, it is often the case that a decision which is rendered by one individual in consideration of the impartiality of the law, is regarded as prejudiced by others.

Therefore, after having diligently inspected the four types of this vice which we enumerated above,[190] may your Beatitude

---

[190] That is, in chapter one.

deign to mercifully instruct me with a decree determining who among the guilty must be irrevocably cast from ecclesiastical order, and who, in preference of discretion, may be mercifully permitted to remain in this office. Regarding which form of the above-mentioned vices and number of accomplices may an offender be allowed to continue in ecclesiastical dignity, and for which form and number of accomplices with whom he was soiled is he to be compelled to cease from those duties?[191] Thus many who are laboring under the same ignorance may be instructed by that which is directed to one, as the light of your authority dispels the darkness of our uncertainty, and, so to speak, the plow of the Apostolic See radically uproots the sprout of all error from the field of wavering conscience.

May almighty God grant, O most reverend father, that in the time of your apostolate the monster of this vice may utterly perish, and the condition of the prostrate Church might everywhere be restored in accordance with the laws of its youth.

---

[191] As is clear from the rest of Damian's work as well as the response of Pope St. Leo IX, Damian is not implying that some clergy who continue to engage in these vices should be allowed to continue in the priesthood, but rather that they might be permitted to return to the priesthood after repenting and performing rigorous penances mandated by canon law.

ABBREVIATIONS

DR   Douay-Rheims Bible (1582–1610).

DRC   Douay-Rheims-Challoner Bible (1749–1752).

D   *Enchiridion symbolorum*, ed. H. J. D. Denzinger (1857ff).

Gaetani   *Beati Petri Damiani Opera Omnia*, ed Constantino Gaetani, 4 vols. (Paris, 1642).

Hefele   *A History of the Christian Councils from the Original Documents to the Close of the Council of Nicea, A.D. 325*, 2nd rev. ed., ed. Charles J. Hefele, trans. William R. Clark (Edinburgh, 1872).

Mansi   *Sacrorum Conciliorum Nova et Amplissima Collectio*, ed. Joannes Mansi (Florence, 1759).

Percival   *The Seven Ecumenical Councils of the Undivided Church*, ed. Henry R. Percival (Oxford: James Parker, 1900).

PL   *Patrologia Series Latina*, ed. J. P. Migne (Paris, 1844–1855).

Reindel   Peter Damian, *Die Briefe des Petrus Damiani*,
            4 vols, ed. Kurt Reindel (Munich: Monunmenta
            Germaniae Historica, 1983–1993).

SELECT BIBLIOGRAPHY

Bareille, Chanoine Georges. "DAMIEN (Saint Pierre)." In *Dictionnaire de Theologie Catholique*, vol. 4, col. 40–54. Paris: Librairie Letouzey et Ane, 1939.

Baronius, Caesar. *Annales Ecclesiastici.* Paris: Barri-Ducis, 1869.

Biron, Réginald. *St. Pierre Damien (1007–1072)*. 20th ed. Paris: Lecoffre, 1908.

Blum, Owen. *St. Peter Damian: His Teaching on the Spiritual Life.* Washington: Catholic University of America Press, 1947.

Boswell, John. *Christianity, Social Tolerance, and Homosexuality.* Chicago: University of Chicago Press, 1980.

Brebier, Louis. "Peter Damian." In *The Catholic Encyclopedia*, vol. 11, 764–766. New York: Robert Appleton Company, 1908.

Delarc, Odon Jean Marie. *Un Pape Alsacien: essai historique sur Saint Léon IX et son temps.* Paris, 1876.

Hefele, Charles Joseph. *A History of the Christian Councils from the Original Documents to the Close of the Council of Nicea, A.D. 325.* 2nd, rev. ed. Edited and translated by William R. Clark. Edinburgh, 1872.

Holopainen, Toivo J. "Peter Damian." In *The Stanford Encyclopedia of Philosophy*, Winter 2012 ed., at plato. stanford.edu.

Leclercq, Jean. *Saint Pierre Damien, ermite et homme d'eglise.* Rome: Edizioni di storia e letteratura, 1960.

Mann, Horace K. *The Lives of the Popes in the Middle Ages.* 12 vols. St. Louis: B. Herder, 1902.

McCready, William David. *Odiosa sanctitas: St. Peter Damian, simony, and reform.* Toronto: Pontifical Institute of Medieval Studies, 2011.

Olsen, Glenn W. *Sodomites, Effeminates, Hermaphrodites, and Androgynes.* Toronto: Pontifical Institute of Medieval Studies, 2011.

Percival, Henry R., ed. *A Select Library of the Nicene and Post-Nicene Fathers of the Christian Church, Second Series.* Vol. XIV, *The Seven Ecumenical Councils of the Undivided Church.* Oxford: James Parker & Co., 1900.

Peter Damian. *Book of Gomorrah: An Eleventh-Century Treatise against Clerical Homosexual Practices.* Translated by Pierre J. Payer. Waterloo, Ontario: Wilfrid Laurier University Press, 1982.

―――. *Die Briefe des Petrus Damiani*, vols. 1–4. Edited by Kurt Reindel. Munich: Monumenta Germaniae Historica, 1983–1993.

―――. *The Letters of Peter Damian.* Translated by Owen J. Blum. Washington: Catholic University of America Press, 1990.

————. *Opera Omnia in Quatuor Tomos Distributa, Collecta ac Agumentis et Notationibus Illustrata.* 4 vols. Edited by Constantine Gaetani. Paris, 1642.

Ranft, Patricia. *The Theology of Peter Damian : 'Let Your Life Always Serve As A Witness.'* Washington, D.C.: Catholic University of America Press, 2012.

Ryan, John J. *Saint Peter Damiani and his canonical sources.* Toronto: Pontifical Institute of Medieval Studies, 1956.

ABOUT THE TRANSLATOR

Matthew Cullinan Hoffman's award-winning articles have appeared hundreds of times in dozens of major newspapers, magazines, and news services, including the *Wall Street Journal, London Sunday Times, Detroit News, LifeSite News, Catholic World Report,* and the *National Catholic Register.* He has been a Latin America correspondent with *LifeSite News* since 2007, and oversaw the creation and initial direction of Notifam, LSN's Spanish and Portuguese language service. He is currently a graduate student at Holy Apostles College and Seminary, where he is certified for proficiency in Latin, French, Spanish, Portuguese, and Italian.

Continued from last page:

"An excellent and accurate translation, and the most reliable English Version of the *Liber Gomorrhianus* of Saint Peter Damian (1007-1072). The work of Matthew Hoffman in translating Damian's from Latin into English shows on the technical side a deep study and an intense commitment to this book and to the language of its author—who lived during the High Middle Ages—and on the conceptual side the will to restore to the English speaking world a book that is a fundamental to the history of our Church. Thanks to Matthew Hoffman we can listen to the voice of Peter Damian against sodomy through this masterpiece that is the *Book of Gomorrah*."

—Dr. Michela Ferri
Adjunct Professor of Philosophy
Holy Apostles College

"With this translation, Matthew Hoffman gives a tremendous gift to the Church, at a time when she desperately needs to hear the undiluted truth, spoken with love, even at the risk of offending."

—Fr. Shenan Boquet
President of Human Life International

Continued from back cover:

"At a time when there is a tragic effort in our societies on both sides of the ocean, to consider normal what it is against nature, Matthew Hoffman has to be strongly congratulated for making accessible the *Liber Gomorrhianus* of St. Peter Damian, an important Doctor of the Church ... The translation is clear and well-articulated, rendering the book in elegant English."

—Msgr. Ignacio Barreiro, J.D., S.T.D.,
Executive Director of the Rome Office
of Human Life International

"Peter Damian's *Liber Gomorrhianus* tackles sexual immorality among Christians, especially clergy and religious, with shocking frankness. Yet his unwavering condemnation of sexual impurity appears alongside his laments over the souls of those who have fallen into impurity and exhortations that they rise again. Scholars of ecclesiastical history and a more general audience comprised of those who wonder how today's struggles with sexual purity may be illuminated by a preeminent reformer of the Medieval period will appreciate this readily accessible and faithful translation of the *Liber Gomorrhianus*."

—Dr. Daniel Van Slyke, Ph.D., S.T.L.
Associate Professor of Theology
Holy Apostles College and Seminary

(Continued on previous page.)

62728526R00112

Made in the USA
Lexington, KY
15 April 2017